CAT TALES

CLASSIC STORIES
FROM FAVORITE WRITERS

Introduction by Cleveland Amory

With Photographs by Robin Upward

WINGS BOOKS
New York • Avenel, New Jersey

To my grandmother Celia, my guardian angel,
for her wisdom and faith. God bless her.

ACKNOWLEDGMENTS

I wish to extend my loving thanks to Elizabeth Botwright-Becker. She patiently and resourcefully styled many of the photographs, and her gift with my feline subjects was invaluable. I am grateful also to Lyle Webster for his unwavering friendship and steady support. My photography mentor, Hank Wessel, taught me to previsualize my images and awoke in me an important creative freedom. Michael A. D'Asaro, my fencing master, helped me by believing that whatever I set out to do, I could do. My parents were there when I most needed them. I am grateful also to Pamela Prince and Carol Hacker. Rita Aero and Esther Mitgang saw my photographs and created a book around them. And, special thanks to all of the cats who convinced their owners to let them pose for this book.

Grateful acknowledgment is made for permission to reprint the following works:
"The King of the Cats" from *The Selected Works of Stephen Vincent Benét*. Published by Holt, Rinehart & Winston, Inc. Copyright 1933 by Stephen Vincent Benét. Copyright renewed © 1963 by Thomas C. Benét, Stephanie B. Mahin and Rachel Benét Lewis. Reprinted by permission of Brandt & Brandt Literary Agents, Inc.
"The Long-Cat" from *Creatures Great and Small* by Colette. Copyright © 1952 by Farrar, Straus and Cudahy. Reprinted by permission of Farrar, Straus and Giroux, Inc.
"A Persian Tale" from *Forty Good Morning Tales* by Rose Fyleman. By permission of the Society of Authors as the literary representatives of the Estate of Rose Fyleman.
"Tobermory" from *The Complete Short Stories of Saki* by H. H. Munro. Copyright 1930, renewed © 1958 by The Viking Press, Inc. All rights reserved. Reprinted by permission of Viking Penguin, a division of Penguin Books USA Inc.
"Little White King" by Marguerite Steen. By permission of the Estate of Marguerite Steen.

This 1996 edition is published by Wings Books, a division of Random House Value Publishing, Inc., 40 Engelhard Avenue, Avenel, New Jersey 07001, by arrangement with Viking Penguin, a division of Penguin Books USA Inc.

Random House
New York • Toronto • London • Sydney • Auckland

Printed and bound in China

Library of Congress Cataloging-in-Publication Data

Cat tales : classic stories from favorite writers / with photographs
by Robin Upward ; introduction by Cleveland Amory.
p.   cm.
Contents: The king of the cats / Stephen Vincent Benét — The
Cheshire cat / Lewis Carroll — Who is to blame? / Anton Chekhov —
The long-cat / Colette — A Persian tale / Rose Fyleman — Puss in
boots / Charles Perrault — Tobermory / Saki — Little white king /
Marguerite Steen — Dick Baker's cat / Mark Twain — The paradise of
cats / Emile Zola.
ISBN 0-517-14853-6 (hardcover)
1. Cats—Fiction. 2. Short stories. I. Upward, Robin.
[PN6120.95.C3C38   1996]   95-41974
808.83'936—dc20   CIP

8 7 6 5 4 3 2 1

CONTENTS

CLEVELAND AMORY

The literature of the cat is vast. My friend Gertrude Zeehandelaar, of the Cat Book Center, estimates it worldwide at over twenty thousand volumes. And, if this literature is, like the cat himself — at least, compared to the horse, the bird, and the dog — a relative Johnny-come-lately, it is nonetheless rapidly overtaking all other individual animal literatures.

This literature also takes, again like the cat himself, some extraordinarily individual byways. An example of this recently crossed my desk in the form of a book entitled, of all things, *A Cat's Guide to Shakespeare.*

At first I wasn't sure whether it was a book for people who wanted to be guided through Shakespeare through the eyes of a cat or whether it was a book about Shakespeare for cats. Upon opening it, however, I found that it was neither — it was an art book containing drawings of cats, illustrating such Shakespearian quotations as *The Taming of the Shrew*'s "And thereby hangs a tale" and *Julius Caesar*'s "I am indeed, sir, a surgeon to old shoes."

In point of fact, cat literature has its beginnings in fables — which exist in the folklore of almost every country. And while most of these are humorous, their primary purpose, from Aesop to La Fontaine, was to demonstrate a moral principle.

To have chosen the cat for such a task would seem, however, an exercise in futility. Indeed, I am indebted to another friend, Jack Smith of the Los Angeles *Times,* for the definitive statement on this ticklish point: "I can honestly say," Mr. Smith wrote, "that I never knew a moral cat." I take, of course, some umbrage at this. My cat, Polar Bear, has a kind of morality which is, I believe, in many ways more honest than mine. The

New England conscience, I have often said, does not stop you from doing what you shouldn't — it just stops you from enjoying it. Polar Bear's conscience, on the other hand, not only doesn't stop him from doing what he shouldn't, it also doesn't stop him from enjoying it thoroughly.

Morality aside, to French literature goes first credit for the promotion of the cat to something beyond fables. And this, as I tried to make clear in *The Cat Who Came for Christmas*, is entirely as it should be, if for no other reason than because it was Théophile Gautier, the French poet and novelist, who, albeit immodestly, reduced the contest to nationalistic dimensions. "Only a Frenchman," he wrote, "could understand the fine and subtle qualities of the cat."

Whether true or not, a veritable host of celebrated French authors — Montaigne, Chateaubriand, Beaudelaire, Balzac, Alexandre Dumas *père* and *fils*, Cocteau, and others — did their best to prove it so. And thus in this collection, *Cat Tales*, it is entirely fitting that, of ten selections, three are from French pens.

The first, from Colette, is entitled in English "The Long-Cat," and it embodies Colette's lifelong belief, which early in life she described in *The Tendrils of the Vine*: "By associating with the cat, one only risks becoming richer." The second selection, from the famed fairy-tale collector Charles Perrault, goes back to the fable format — and Monsieur Perrault gives us, for once, a fable in which the cat is neither deceiver nor villain but, clearly, the hero. The third French offering, from Émile Zola, also gives us a fable — in this one the indoor Fat Cat learns from the outdoor Tom of the perils of freedom.

Second only to France in the literature of the cat is England, and *Cat Tales* contains the work of no fewer than four British authors. The first offering is the familiar Cheshire, from Lewis Carroll's *Alice in Wonderland* — the cat who is at one time "a grin without a cat" and, at another, a cat Alice finds no use speaking to "till its ears have

come, or at least one of them." My favorite character is still the executioner who, ordered to cut off its head, refuses to do so, arguing in typical British fashion that "you couldn't cut off a head unless there was a body to cut it off from; that he had never had to do such a thing before, and he wasn't going to begin at *his* time of life."

Two other British selections — one from the late Rose Fyleman, an old-time *Punch* writer, the other from Marguerite Steen, who wrote her first novel at the age of eight — tell in one case the story of how the first Persian kitten came into the world and, in the other, a story with a twist at the end you cannot possibly haved guessed.

The fourth British selection, from the late H. H. Munro, better known as Saki, is the classic "Tobermory." This is the story of a man who discovers he can teach animals to speak and, working with cats, which he describes as, "those wonderful creatures who have assimilated themselves so marvelously with our civilization while retaining all their highly developed feral instincts," then manages with the cat Tobermory an unforgettable feral attack on an entire English house party.

There is here too a Russian selection — from the renowned Anton Chekhov. The age-old cat-and-mouse story, it bears, from first sentence to last, the indelible Chekhovian stamp.

Finally, there are two American selections. The first, which leads off this volume, is from the late Stephen Vincent Benét, author of *John Brown's Body*, the book that I consider the best published in this country in my lifetime. In any case, the selection here is certainly one of the most intriguing cat stories ever told. There are, after all, werewolves — why not were-cats?

The second American selection is from the one and only Mark Twain. And that too is as it should be. For it was the peerless Mark who left us what is my very favorite cat quotation in all literature.

vi

"If," he said, "man could be crossed with a cat, it would improve man but it would deteriorate the cat."

THE KING OF THE CATS

"But, my *dear*," said Mrs. Culverin, with a tiny gasp, "you can't actually mean — a *tail!*"

Mrs. Dingle nodded impressively. "Exactly. I've actually seen him. Twice. Paris, of course, and then, a command appearance at Rome — we were in the royal box. He conducted — my dear, you've never heard such effects from an orchestra — and, my dear," she hesitated slightly, "he conducted *with it.*"

"How perfectly, fascinatingly too horrid for words!" said Mrs. Culverin in a dazed but greedy voice. "We *must* have him to dinner as soon as he comes over — he is coming over, isn't he?"

"The twelfth," said Mrs. Dingle with a gleam in her eyes. "The New Symphony people have asked him to be guest conductor for three special concerts — I do hope you can dine with *us* some night while he's here

BENÉT

— he'll be very busy, of course — but he's promised to give us what time he can spare."

"Oh, thank you, dear," said Mrs. Culverin abstractedly, her last raid upon Mrs. Dingle's pet British novelist still fresh in her mind. "You're always so delightfully hospitable — but you mustn't wear yourself out — the rest of us must do *our* part — I know Harry and myself would be only too glad to —"

"That's very sweet of you, darling." Mrs. Dingle also remembered the larceny of the British novelist. "But we're just going to give Monsieur Tibault — sweet name, isn't it! They say he's descended from the Tybalt in *Romeo and Juliet* and that's why he doesn't like Shakespeare — we're just going to give Monsieur Tibault the simplest sort of time — a little reception after his first concert, perhaps. He hates," she looked around the table, "large, mixed parties. And then, of course, his — er — little idiosyncrasy." She coughed delicately. "It makes him feel a trifle shy with strangers."

"But I don't understand yet, Aunt Emily," said Tommy Brooks, Mrs. Dingle's nephew. "Do you really mean this Tibault bozo has a tail? Like a monkey and everything?"

"Tommy dear," said Mrs. Culverin crushingly, "in the first place Monsieur Tibault is not a bozo — he is a very distinguished musician — the finest conductor in Europe. And in the second place —"

"He has." Mrs. Dingle was firm. "He has a tail. He conducts with it."

"Oh, but honestly!" said Tommy, his ears pinkening. "I mean — of course, if you say so, Aunt Emily, I'm sure he has — but still, it sounds pretty steep, if you know what I mean! How about it, Professor Tatto?"

Professor Tatto cleared his throat. "Tck," he said, putting his fingertips together cautiously. "I shall be very anxious to see this Monsieur Tibault. For myself, I have never observed a genuine specimen of *homo caudatus,* so I should be inclined to doubt, and yet... In the Middle Ages, for instance, the belief in men — er — tailed or with caudal appendages of some sort, was both widespread and, as far as we can gather, well founded. As late as the

2

eighteenth century, a Dutch sea captain with some character for veracity recounts the discovery of a pair of such creatures in the Island of Formosa. They were in a low state of civilization, I believe, but the appendages in question were quite distinct. And in 1860 Dr. Grimbrook, the English surgeon, claims to have treated no less than three African natives with short but evident tails — though his testimony rests upon his unsupported word. After all, the thing is not impossible, though doubtless unusual. Web feet — rudimentary gills — these occur with some frequency. The appendix we have with us always. The chain of our descent from the ape-like form is by no means complete. For that matter," he beamed around the table, "what can we call the last few vertebrae of the normal spine but the beginnings of a rudimentary tail? Oh, yes — yes — it's possible — quite — that in an extraordinary case — a reversion to type — a survival —"

"I told you so," said Mrs. Dingle triumphantly. *"Isn't* it fascinating? Isn't it, Princess?"

The Princess Vivrakanarda's eyes, blue as a field of larkspur, fathomless as the center of heaven, rested lightly for a moment on Mrs. Dingle's excited countenance.

"Ve-ry fascinating," she said, in a voice like stroked, golden velvet. "I should like ve-ry much to meet this Monsieur Tibault."

"Well, *I* hope he breaks his neck!" said Tommy Brooks under his breath — but nobody ever paid much attention to Tommy.

Nevertheless, as the time for Monsieur Tibault's arrival in these states drew nearer and nearer, people in general began to wonder whether the Princess had spoken quite truthfully — for there was no doubt of the fact that, up till then, she had been the unique sensation of the season — and you know what social lions and lionesses are.

It was a Siamese season, and genuine Siamese were at quite as much of a premium as Russian accents had been in the quaint old days when the Chauve-Souris was a novelty. The Siamese Art Theater, imported at terrific expense, was playing to packed houses at the Century

Theater. *Gushuptzgu*, an epic novel of Siamese farm life, in nineteen closely printed volumes, had just been awarded the Nobel Prize. Prominent pet-and-newt dealers reported no cessation in the appalling demand for Siamese cats. And upon the crest of the wave of interest in things Siamese the Princess Vivrakanarda poised with the elegant nonchalance of a Hawaiian water baby upon his surfboard. She was indispensable. She was incomparable. She was everywhere.

Youthful, enormously wealthy, allied on one hand to the royal family of Siam and on the other to the Cabots (and yet with the first eighteen of her twenty-one years shrouded from speculation in a golden zone of mystery), the mingling of races in her had produced an exotic beauty as distinguished as it was strange. She moved with a feline, effortless grace, and her skin was as if it had been gently powdered with tiny grains of the purest gold — yet the blueness of her eyes, set just a trifle slantingly, was as pure and startling as the sea on the rocks of Maine. Her brown hair fell to her knees — she had been offered extraordinary sums by the Master Barbers' Protective Association to have it shingled. Straight as a waterfall tumbling over brown rocks, it had a vague perfume of sandalwood and suave spices and held tints of rust and the sun. She did not talk very much — but then she did not have to; her voice had an odd, small, melodious huskiness that haunted the mind. She lived alone and was reputed to be very lazy — at least it was known that she slept during most of the day — but at night she bloomed like a moonflower, and a depth came into her eyes.

It was no wonder that Tommy Brooks fell in love with her. The wonder was that she let him. There was nothing exotic or distinguished about Tommy — he was just one of those pleasant, normal young men who seem created to carry on the bond business by reading the newspapers in the University Club during most of the day, and can always be relied upon to fill an unexpected hole in a dinner party. It is true that the Princess could hardly be said to do more than tolerate any of her suitors — no one had ever seen those aloof and arrogant eyes enliven at the entrance of any male. But she seemed to be able to tolerate Tommy a little more

5

than the rest — and that young man's infatuated daydreams were beginning to be beset by smart solitaires and imaginary apartments on Park Avenue when the famous Monsieur Tibault conducted his first concert at Carnegie Hall.

Tommy Brooks sat beside the Princess. The eyes he turned upon her were eyes of longing and love, but her face was as impassive as a Benda mask, and the only remark she made during the preliminary bustlings was that there seemed to be a number of people in the audience. But Tommy was relieved, if anything, to find her even a little more aloof than usual, for, ever since Mrs. Culverin's dinner party, a vague disquiet as to the possible impression which this Tibault creature might make upon her had been growing in his mind. It shows his devotion that he was present at all. To a man whose simple Princetonian nature found in "Just a Little Love, a Little Kiss," the quintessence of musical art, the average symphony was a positive torture, and he looked forward to the evening's program itself with a grim, brave smile.

"Ssh!" said Mrs. Dingle breathlessly. "He's coming!" It seemed to the startled Tommy as if he were suddenly back in the trenches under a heavy barrage, as Monsieur Tibault made his entrance to a perfect bombardment of applause.

Then the enthusiastic noise was sliced off in the middle, and a gasp took its place — a vast, windy sigh, as if every person in that multitude had suddenly said "Ah!" For the papers had not lied about him. The tail was there.

They called him theatric — but how well he understood the uses of theatricalism! Dressed in unrelieved black from head to foot (the black dress shirt had been a special token of Mussolini's esteem), he did not walk on, he strolled, leisurely, easily, aloofly, the famous tail curled nonchalantly about one wrist — a suave, black panther lounging through a summer garden with that little mysterious weave of the head that panthers have when they pad behind bars — the glittering darkness of his eyes unmoved by any surprise or elation. He nodded, twice in regal acknowledgment, as the clapping reached an apogee of frenzy. To Tommy there was something dreadfully reminiscent of the Princess in the way he nodded.

Then he turned to his orchestra.

A second and louder gasp went up from the audience at this point, for, as he turned, the tip of that incredible tail twined with dainty carelessness into some hidden pocket and produced a black baton. But Tommy did not even notice. He was looking at the Princess instead.

She had not even bothered to clap, at first, but now.... Poor Tommy had never seen her moved like this, never. She was not applauding, her hands were clenched in her lap, but her whole body was rigid, rigid as a steel bar, and the blue flowers of her eyes were bent upon the figure of Monsieur Tibault in a terrible concentration. The pose of her entire figure was so still and intense that for an instant Tommy had the lunatic idea that any moment she might leap from her seat beside him as lightly as a moth, and land, with no sound, at Monsieur Tibault's side to — yes — to rub her proud head against his coat in worship. Even Mrs. Dingle would notice in a moment.

"Princess —" he said, in a horrified whisper, "Princess —"

Slowly the tenseness of her body relaxed, her eyes veiled again, she grew calm.

"Yes, Tommy?" she said, in her usual voice, but there was still something about her....

"Nothing, only — oh, hang — he's starting!" said Tommy, as Monsieur Tibault, his hands loosely clasped before him, turned and *faced* the audience. His eyes dropped; his tail switched once impressively, then gave three little preliminary taps with his baton on the floor.

Seldom has Gluck's overture to *Iphigenia in Aulis* received such an ovation. But it was not until the Eighth Symphony that the hysteria of the audience reached its climax. Never before had the New Symphony been played so superbly — and certainly never before had it been led with such genius. Three prominent conductors in the audience were sobbing with the despairing admiration of envious children toward the close, and at least one was heard to offer wildly ten thousand dollars to a well-known facial surgeon there present for a shred of evidence that

7

tails of some variety could by any stretch of science be grafted upon a normally decaudate form. There was no doubt about it — no mortal hand and arm, be they ever so dexterous, could combine the delicate elan and powerful grace displayed in every gesture of Monsieur Tibault's tail.

A sable staff, it dominated the brasses like a flicker of black lightning; an ebon, elusive whip, it drew the last exquisite breath of melody from the woodwinds and ruled the stormy strings like a magician's rod. Monsieur Tibault bowed and bowed again — roar after roar of frenzied admiration shook the hall to its foundations — and when he finally staggered, exhausted, from the platform, the president of the Wednesday Sonata Club was only restrained by force from flinging her ninety-thousand-dollar string of pearls after him in an excess of aesthetic appreciation. New York had come and seen — and New York was conquered. Mrs. Dingle was immediately besieged by reporters, and Tommy Brooks looked forward to the "little party" at which he was to meet the new hero of the hour with feelings only a little less lugubrious than those that would have come to him just before taking his seat in the electric chair.

The meeting between his princess and Monsieur Tibault was worse and better than he expected. Better because, after all, they did not say much to each other — and worse because it seemed to him, somehow, that some curious kinship of mind between them made words unnecessary. They were certainly the most distinguished-looking couple in the room, as he bent over her hand. "So darlingly foreign, both of them, and yet so different," babbled Mrs. Dingle — but Tommy couldn't agree.

They were very different, yes — the dark, lithe stranger with that bizarre appendage tucked carelessly in his pocket, and the blue-eyed, brown-haired girl. But that difference only accentuated what they had in common — something in the way they moved, in the suavity of their gestures, in the set of their eyes. Something deeper, even, than race. He tried to puzzle it out — then, looking around at the others, he had a flash of revelation. It was as if that couple

were foreign, indeed — not only to New York but to all common humanity. As if they were polite guests from a different star.

Tommy did not have a happy evening, on the whole. But his mind worked slowly, and it was not until much later that the mad suspicion came upon him full force.

Perhaps he is not to be blamed for his lack of immediate comprehension. The next few weeks were weeks of bewildered misery for him. It was not that the Princess's attitude toward him had changed — she was just as tolerant of him as before; but Monsieur Tibault was always there. He had a faculty of appearing as out of thin air — he walked, for all his height, as lightly as a butterfly — and Tommy grew to hate that faintest shuffle on the carpet that announced his presence as he had never hated the pound of the guns.

And then, hang it all, the man was so smooth, so infernally, unruffably smooth! He was never out of temper, never embarrassed. He treated Tommy with the extreme of urbanity, and yet his eyes mocked, deep down, and Tommy could do nothing. And gradually, the Princess became more and more drawn to this stranger, in a soundless communion that found little need for speech — and that, too, Tommy saw and hated, and that, too, he could not mend.

He began to be haunted not only by Monsieur Tibault in the flesh but by Monsieur Tibault in the spirit. He slept badly, and when he slept he dreamed — of Monsieur Tibault, a man no longer, but a shadow, a specter, the limber ghost of an animal whose words came purringly between sharp little pointed teeth. There was certainly something odd about the whole shape of the fellow — his fluid ease, the mold of his head, even the cut of his fingernails — but just what it was escaped Tommy's intensest cogitation. And when he did put his finger on it at length, at first he refused to believe.

A pair of petty incidents decided him, finally, against all reason. He had gone to Mrs. Dingle's, one winter afternoon, hoping to find the Princess. She was out with his aunt, but was expected back for tea, and he wandered idly into the library to wait. He was just about to switch on the lights, for the library was always dark even in summer, when he heard a sound of light breathing that seemed to come from the leather couch in the corner. He approached it cautiously and dimly made out the form of Monsieur Tibault, curled up on the couch, peacefully asleep.

The sight annoyed Tommy so that he swore under his breath and was back near the door on his way out, when the feeling we all know and hate, the feeling that eyes we cannot see are watching us, arrested him. He turned back — Monsieur Tibault had not moved a muscle of his body, to all appearance — but his eyes were open now. And those eyes were black and human no longer. They were green — Tommy could have sworn it — and he could have sworn that they had no bottom and gleamed like little emeralds in the dark. It lasted only a moment, for Tommy pressed the light button automatically — and there was Monsieur Tibault, his normal self, yawning a little but urbanely apologetic, but it gave Tommy time to think. Nor did what happened a trifle later increase his peace of mind.

They had lit a fire and were talking in front of it — by now, Tommy hated Monsieur Tibault so thoroughly that he felt that odd yearning for his company that often occurs in such cases. Monsieur Tibault was telling some anecdote, and Tommy was hating him worse than ever for basking with such obvious enjoyment in the heat of the flames and the ripple of his own voice.

Then they heard the street door open, and Monsieur Tibault jumped up — and, jumping, caught one sock on a sharp corner of the brass fire rail and tore it open in a jagged flap. Tommy looked down mechanically at the tear — a second's glance, but enough — for Monsieur Tibault, for the first time in Tommy's experience, lost his temper completely. He swore violently in some spitting, foreign tongue — his face distorted suddenly — he clapped his hand over his sock. Then, glaring furiously at Tommy, he fairly sprang from the room, and Tommy could hear him scaling the stairs in long, agile bounds. Tommy sank into a chair, careless for once of the fact that he heard the Princess's light laugh in the hall. He didn't want

to see the Princess. He didn't want to see anybody. There had been something revealed when Monsieur Tibault had torn that hole in his sock — and it was not the skin of a man. Tommy had caught a glimpse of — black plush. Black velvet. And then had come Monsieur Tibault's sudden explosion of fury. Good *Lord* — did the man wear black velvet stockings under his ordinary socks? Or could he — could he — but here Tommy held his fevered head in his hands.

He went to Professor Tatto that evening with hypothetical questions, but as he did not dare confide his real suspicions to the professor, the hypothetical answers he received served only to confuse him the more. Then he thought of Billy Strang. Billy was a good sort, and his mind had a turn for the bizarre. Billy might be able to help.

He couldn't get hold of Billy for three days, and lived through the interval in a fever of impatience. But finally they had dinner together at Billy's apartment, where his queer books were, and Tommy was able to blurt out the whole disordered jumble of his suspicions.

Billy listened without interrupting until Tommy was quite through. Then he pulled at his pipe. "But, my dear man —" he said protestingly.

"Oh, I know — I know," said Tommy, and waved his hands, "I know I'm crazy — you needn't tell me that — but I tell you, the man's a cat all the same — no, I don't see how he could be, but he is — why, hang it, in the first place, everybody knows he's got a *tail!*"

"Even so," said Billy Strang, puffing. "Oh, my dear Tommy, I don't doubt you saw, or think you saw, everything you say. But, even so..." He shook his head.

"But what about those other birds, werewolves and things?" said Tommy.

Billy looked dubious. "We-ll," he admitted, "you've got me there, of course. At least — a tailed man *is* possible. And the yarns about werewolves go back far enough so that — well, *I* wouldn't say there aren't or haven't been werewolves — but then I'm willing to believe more things than most people. But a werecat — or a man that's a cat and a cat that's a man — honestly, Tommy —"

"If I don't get some real advice I'll go clean off my hinge. For heaven's sake, tell me something to *do!*"

"Lemme think," said Billy. "First, you're pizen-sure this man is —"

"A cat. Yeah," and Tommy nodded violently.

"Check. And second — if it doesn't hurt your feelings, Tommy — you're afraid this girl you're in love with has — er — at least a streak of — felinity — in her — and so she's drawn to him?"

"Oh, Lord, Billy, if only I knew!"

"Well — er — suppose she really is, too, you know — would you still be keen on her?"

"I'd marry her if she turned into a dragon every Wednesday!" said Tommy fervently.

Billy smiled. "Hmm," he said, "then the obvious thing to do is to get rid of this Monsieur Tibault. Lemme think."

He thought about two pipes full, while Tommy sat on pins and needles. Then, finally, he burst out laughing.

"What's so darn funny?" said Tommy aggrievedly.

"Nothing, Tommy, only I've just thought of a stunt — something so blooming crazy — but if he is — hmm — what you think he is — it *might* work." And, going to the bookcase, he took down a book.

"If you think you're going to quiet my nerves by reading me a bedtime story —"

"Shut up, Tommy, and listen to this — if you really want to get rid of your feline friend."

"What is it?" asked Tommy gloomily.

"Book of Agnes Repplier's. About cats. Listen.

" 'There is also a Scandinavian version of the ever famous story which Sir Walter Scott told to Washington Irving, which Monk Lewis told to Shelley, and which, in one form or another, we find embodied in the folklore of every land' — now, Tommy, pay attention — 'the story of the traveler who saw within a ruined abbey, a procession of cats, lowering into a

13

grave a little coffin with a crown upon it. Filled with horror, he hastened from the spot; but when he had reached his destination he could not forbear relating to a friend the wonder he had seen. Scarcely had the tale been told when his friend's cat, who lay curled up tranquilly by the fire, sprang to its feet, cried out, "Then I am the King of the Cats!" and disappeared in a flash up the chimney.'

"Well?" said Billy, shutting the book.

"By gum!" said Tommy, staring. "By gum! Do you really think there's a chance?"

"I think we're both in the booby hatch. But if you want to try it —"

"Try it! I'll spring it on him the next time I see him. But — listen — I can't make it in a ruined abbey."

"Oh, use your imagination! Make it Central Park. Tell it as if it happened to you — seeing the funeral procession and all that. You can lead into it somehow — let's see, some general line — oh, yes — 'Strange, isn't it, how fact so often copies fiction? Why, only yesterday . . .' See?"

"Strange, isn't it, how fact so often copies fiction," repeated Tommy dutifully. "Why only yesterday . . ."

"I happened to be strolling through Central Park when I saw something very odd."

"I happened to be strolling through — here, gimme that book!" said Tommy. "I want to learn the rest of it by heart!"

Mrs. Dingle's farewell dinner to the famous Monsieur Tibault, on the occasion of his departure for his Western tour, was looked forward to with the greatest expectations. Not only could everybody be there, including the Princess Vivrakanarda, but Mrs. Dingle, a hinter if there ever was one, had let it be known that at this dinner an announcement of very unusual interest to Society might be made. So everyone, for once, was almost on time, except for Tommy. He was at least fifteen minutes early, for he wanted to have speech with his aunt alone. Unfortunately, however, he had hardly taken off his overcoat when she was whispering

some news in his ear so rapidly that he found it difficult to understand a word of it.

"And you mustn't breathe it to a soul!" she ended, beaming. "That is, not before the announcement — I think we'll have *that* with the salad — people never pay very much attention to salad —"

"Breathe what, Aunt Emily?" said Tommy, confused.

"The Princess, darling — the dear Princess and Monsieur Tibault — they just got engaged this afternoon, dear things! Isn't it *fascinating?*"

"Yeah," said Tommy, and started to walk blindly through the nearest door. His aunt restrained him.

"Not there, dear, not in the library. You can congratulate them later. They're just having a sweet little moment alone there now." And she turned away to harry the butler, leaving Tommy stunned.

But his chin came up after a moment. He wasn't beaten yet.

"Strange, isn't it, how often fact copies fiction?" he repeated to himself in dull mnemonics, and, as he did so, he shook his fist at the closed library door.

Mrs. Dingle was wrong, as usual. The Princess and Monsieur Tibault were not in the library — they were in the conservatory, as Tommy discovered when he wandered aimlessly past the glass doors.

He didn't mean to look, and after a second he turned away. But that second was enough.

Tibault sat in a chair and she was crouched on a stool at his side, while his hand, softly, smoothly, stroked her brown hair. Black cat and Siamese kitten. Her face was hidden from Tommy, but he could see Tibault's face. And he could hear.

They were not talking, but there was a sound between them. A warm and contented sound like the murmur of giant bees in a hollow tree — a golden, musical rumble, deep-throated, that came from Tibault's lips and was answered by hers — a golden purr.

Somehow Tommy found himself back in the drawing room, shaking hands with Mrs. Culverin, who said frankly that she had seldom seen him look so pale.

The first two courses of the dinner passed Tommy like dreams, but Mrs. Dingle's cellar was notable, and by the middle of the meat course he began to come to himself. He had only one resolve now.

For the next few moments he tried desperately to break into the conversation, but Mrs. Dingle was talking, and even Gabriel will have a time interrupting Mrs. Dingle. At last, though, she paused for breath, and Tommy saw his chance.

"Speaking of that," said Tommy piercingly, without knowing in the least what he was referring to, "speaking of that —"

"As I was saying," said Professor Tatto. But Tommy would not yield. The plates were being taken away. It was time for salad.

"Speaking of that," he said again, so loudly and strangely that Mrs. Culverin jumped, and an awkward hush fell over the table. "Strange, isn't it, how often fact copies fiction?" There, he was started. His voice rose even higher. "Why, only today I was strolling through..." and, word for word, he repeated his lesson. He could see Tibault's eyes glowing at him as he described the funeral. He could see the Princess, tense.

He could not have said what he had expected might happen when he came to the end. But it was not bored silence everywhere, to be followed by Mrs. Dingle's acrid, "Well, Tommy, is that *quite* all?"

He slumped back in his chair, sick at heart. He was a fool, and his last resource had failed. Dimly he heard his aunt's voice saying, "Well, then —" and realized that she was about to make the fatal announcement.

But just then Monsieur Tibault spoke.

"One moment, Mrs. Dingle," he said, with extreme politeness, and she was silent. He turned to Tommy.

"You are... positive, I suppose, of what you saw this afternoon, Brooks?" he said in tones of light mockery.

"Absolutely," said Tommy sullenly. "Do you think I'd —"

"Oh, no, no, no," Monsieur Tibault waved the implication aside, "but — such an interesting story — one likes to be sure of the details — and, of course, you *are* sure — *quite* sure — that the kind of crown you describe was on the coffin?"

"Of course," said Tommy, wondering, "but —"

"Then I'm the King of the Cats!" cried Monsieur Tibault in a voice of thunder, and, even, as he cried it, the house lights blinked — there was the soft thud of an explosion that seemed muffled in cotton wool from the minstrel galley — and the scene was lit for a second by an obliterating and painful burst of light that vanished in an instant and was succeeded by heavy, blinding clouds of white, pungent smoke.

"Oh, those *horrid* photographers," came Mrs. Dingle's voice in a melodious wail. "I *told* them not to take the flashlight picture till dinner was over, and now they've taken it *just* as I was nibbling lettuce!"

Someone tittered a little nervously. Someone coughed. Then, gradually, the veils of smoke dislimned and the green and black spots in front of Tommy's eyes died away.

They were blinking at each other like people who have just come out of a cave into brilliant sun. Even yet their eyes stung with the fierceness of that abrupt illumination, and Tommy found it hard to make out the faces across the table from him.

Mrs. Dingle took command of the half-blinded company with her accustomed poise. She rose, glass in hand. "And now, dear friends," she said in a clear voice, "I'm sure all of us are very happy to —" Then she stopped, open-mouthed, an expression of incredulous horror on her features. The lifted glass began to spill its contents on the tablecloth in a little stream of amber. As she spoke she had turned directly to Monsieur Tibault's place at the table — and Monsieur Tibault was no longer there.

Some say there was a bursting flash of fire that disappeared up the chimney — some say it was a giant cat that leaped through the window at a bound, without breaking the glass. Professor Tatto puts it down to a mysterious chemical disturbance operating only over Monsieur Tibault's chair. Be that as it may, one thing is certain: in the instant of fictive darkness which followed the glare of the flashlight, Monsieur Tibault, the great conductor, disappeared forever from mortal sight, tail and all.

Mrs. Culverin swears he was an international burglar and that she was just about to unmask him, but no one who sat at that historic table believes her. No, there are no sound explanations, but Tommy thinks he knows, and he will never be able to pass a cat again without wondering.

Mrs. Tommy is quite of her husband's mind regarding cats — she was Gretchen Woolwine, of Chicago (*you* know the Woolwines!) — for Tommy told her his whole story.

Doubtless it would have been more romantic to relate how Tommy's daring won him his princess — but, unfortunately, it would not be veracious. For the Princess Vivrakanarda, also, is with us no longer. Her nerves, shattered by the spectacular denouement of Mrs. Dingle's dinner, required a sea voyage, and from that voyage she has never returned to America.

Of course, there are the usual stories — one hears of her, a nun in a Siamese convent, or a masked dancer at *Le Jardin de ma Soeur* — one hears that she has been murdered in Patagonia or married in Trebizond — but, as far as can be ascertained, not one of these gaudy fables has the slightest basis in fact. I believe that Tommy, in his heart of hearts, is quite convinced that the sea voyage was only a pretext, and that by some unheard-of means she has managed to rejoin the formidable Monsieur Tibault, in fact, that in some ruined city or subterranean place they reign together now, King and Queen of all the mysterious Kingdom of Cats. But that, of course, is quite impossible.

THE CHESHIRE CAT

The only things in the kitchen that did not sneeze were the cook, and a large cat which was sitting on the hearth and grinning from ear to ear.

"Please, would you tell me," said Alice a little timidly, for she was not quite sure whether it was good manners for her to speak first, "why your cat grins like that?"

"It's a Cheshire cat," said the Duchess, "and that's why. Pig!"

She said the last word with such sudden violence that Alice quite jumped; but she saw in another moment that it was addressed to the baby, and not to her, so she took courage, and went on again:

"I didn't know that Cheshire cats always grinned; in fact, I didn't know that cats *could* grin."

"They all can," said the Duchess; "and most of 'em do."

"I don't know of any that do," Alice said

CARROLL

very politely, feeling quite pleased to have got into a conversation.

"You don't know much," said the Duchess; "and that's a fact."

Alice did not at all like the tone of this remark, and thought it would be as well to introduce some other subject of conversation. While she was trying to fix on one, the cook took the cauldron of soup off the fire, and at once set to work throwing everything within her reach at the Duchess and the baby — the fire-irons came first; then followed a shower of saucepans, plates, and dishes. The Duchess took no notice of them even when they hit her; and the baby was howling so much already, that it was quite impossible to say whether the blows hurt it or not.

"Oh, *please* mind what you're doing!" cried Alice, jumping up and down in an agony of terror. "Oh, there goes his *precious* nose;" as an unusually large saucepan flew close by it, and very nearly carried it off.

"If everybody minded their own business," the Duchess said in a hoarse growl, "the world would go round a deal faster than it does."

"Which would *not* be an advantage," said Alice, who felt very glad to get an opportunity of showing off a little of her knowledge. "Just think what work it would make with the day and night! You see the earth takes twenty-four hours to turn round on its axis —"

"Talking of axes," said the Duchess, "chop off her head!"

Alice glanced rather anxiously at the cook, to see if she meant to take the hint; but the cook was busily engaged in stirring the soup, and did not seem to be listening, so she ventured to go on again: "Twenty-four hours, I *think*; or is it twelve? I —"

"Oh, don't bother *me*," said the Duchess; "I never could abide figures!" And with that she began nursing her child again, singing a sort of lullaby to it as she did so, and giving it a violent shake at the end of every line:

> *"Speak roughly to your little boy,*
> *And beat him when he sneezes:*

He only does it to annoy,
  Because he knows it teases."

Chorus (In which the cook and the baby joined)
"Wow! wow! wow!"

While the Duchess sang the second verse of the song, she kept tossing the baby violently up and down, and the poor little thing howled so, that Alice could hardly hear the words:

"I speak severely to my boy,
  I beat him when he sneezes;
For he can thoroughly enjoy
  The pepper when he pleases!"

Chorus
"Wow! wow! wow!"

"Here! you may nurse it a bit, if you like!" the Duchess said to Alice, flinging the baby at her as she spoke. "I must go and get ready to play croquet with the Queen," and she hurried out of the room. The cook threw a frying-pan after her as she went out, but it just missed her.

Alice caught the baby with some difficulty, as it was a queer-shaped little creature, and held out its arms and legs in all directions, "just like a star-fish," thought Alice. The poor little thing was snorting like a steam-engine when she caught it, and kept doubling itself up and straightening itself out again, so that altogether, for the first minute or two, it was as much as she could do to hold it.

As soon as she made out the proper way of nursing it (which was to twist it up into a sort of knot, and then keep tight hold of its right ear and left foot, so as to prevent its undoing itself), she carried it out into the open air. "If I don't take this child away with me," thought Alice, "they're sure to kill it in a day or two: wouldn't it be murder to leave it behind?" She said the last words out loud, and the little thing grunted in reply (it had left off sneezing by this time). "Don't grunt," said Alice; "that's not at all a proper way of expressing yourself."

The baby grunted again, and Alice looked very anxiously into its face to see what was the matter with it. There could be no doubt that it had a *very* turn-up nose, much more like a snout that a real nose; also its eyes were getting extremely small for a baby: altogether Alice did not like the look of the thing at all. "But perhaps it was only sobbing," she thought, and looked into its eyes again, to see if there were any tears.

No, there were no tears. "If you're going to turn into a pig, my dear," said Alice, seriously, "I'll have nothing more to do with you. Mind now!" The poor little thing sobbed again (or grunted, it was impossible to say which), and they went on for some while in silence.

Alice was just beginning to think to herself, "Now, what am I to do with this creature when I get it home?" when it grunted again, so violently that she looked down into its face in some alarm. This time there could be *no* mistake about it: it was neither more nor less than a pig, and she felt that it would be quite absurd for her to carry it any further.

So she set the little creature down, and felt quite relieved to see it trot away quietly into the wood. "If it had grown up," she said to herself, "it would have made a dreadfully ugly child; but it makes rather a handsome pig, I think." And she began thinking over other children she knew, who might do very well as pigs, and was just saying to herself, "If one only knew the right way to change them —" when she was a little startled by seeing the Cheshire Cat sitting on a bough of a tree a few yards off.

The Cat only grinned when it saw Alice. It looked good-natured, she thought; still it had *very* long claws and a great many teeth, so she felt that it ought to be treated with respect.

"Cheshire Puss," she began, rather timidly, as she did not at all know whether it would like the name: however, it only grinned a little wider. "Come, it's pleased so far," thought Alice, and she went on: "Would you tell me, please, which way I ought to go from here?"

"That depends a good deal on where you want to get to," said the Cat.

"I don't much care where —" said Alice.

"Then it doesn't matter which way you go," said the Cat.

"— so long as I get *somewhere*," Alice added as an explanation.

"Oh, you're sure to do that," said the Cat, "if you only walk long enough."

Alice felt that this could not be denied, so she tried another question: "What sort of people live about here?"

"In *that* direction," the Cat said, waving its right paw round, "lives a Hatter: and in *that* direction," waving the other paw, "lives a March Hare. Visit either you like: they're both mad."

"But I don't want to go among mad people," Alice remarked.

"Oh, but you can't help that," said the Cat; "we're all mad here. I'm mad. You're mad."

"How do you know I'm mad?" said Alice.

"You must be," said the Cat, "or you wouldn't have come here."

Alice didn't think that proved it at all; however, she went on: "And how do you know that you're mad?"

"To begin with," said the Cat, "a dog's not mad. You grant that?"

"I suppose so," said Alice.

"Well, then," the Cat went on, "you see a dog growls when it's angry, and wags its tail when it's pleased. Now *I* growl when I'm pleased, and wag my tail when I'm angry. Therefore, I'm mad."

"I call it purring, not growling," said Alice.

"Call it what you like," said the Cat. "Do you play croquet with the Queen to-day?"

"I should like it very much," said Alice, "but I haven't been invited yet."

"You'll see me there," said the Cat, and vanished.

Alice was not much surprised at this, she was getting so used to queer things happening. While she was looking at the place where it had been, it suddenly appeared again.

"By the by, what became of the baby?" said the Cat. "I'd nearly forgotten to ask."

"It turned into a pig," Alice quietly said, just as if it had come back in a natural way.

"I thought it would," said the Cat, and vanished again.

Alice waited a little, half expecting to see it again, but it did not appear, and after a minute or two she walked on in the direction in which the March Hare was said to live. "I've seen hatters before," she said to herself; "the March Hare will be much the most interesting, and perhaps, as this is May, it won't be raving mad — at least not so mad as it was in March." As she said this, she looked up, and there was the Cat again, sitting on a branch of a tree.

"Did you say pig, or fig?" said the Cat.

"I said pig," replied Alice; "and I wish you wouldn't keep appearing and vanishing so suddenly: you make one quite giddy."

"All right," said the Cat; and this time it vanished quite slowly, beginning with the end of the tail, and ending with the grin, which remained some time after the rest of it had gone.

"Well! I've often seen a cat without a grin," thought Alice; "but a grin without a cat! It's the most curious thing I ever saw in all my life!"

* * *

Alice began to feel very uneasy: to be sure she had not as yet had any dispute with the Queen, but she knew that it might happen any minute, "and then," thought she, "what would become of me? They're dreadfully fond of beheading people here; the great wonder is that there's anyone left alive!"

She was looking about for some way of escape, and wondering whether she could get away without being seen, when she noticed a curious appearance in the air: it puzzled her very much at first, but, after watching it a minute or two, she made it out to be a grin, and she said to herself, "It's the Cheshire Cat: now I shall have somebody to talk to."

"How are you getting on?" said the Cat, as soon as there was mouth enough for it to speak with.

Alice waited till the eyes appeared, and then nodded. "It's no use speaking to it," she thought, "till its ears have come, or at least one of them." In another minute the whole head appeared, and then Alice put down her flamingo, and began an account of the game, feeling very glad she had someone to listen to her. The Cat seemed to think that there was enough of it now in sight, and no more of it appeared.

"I don't think they play at all fairly," Alice began, in rather a complaining tone, "and they all quarrel so dreadfully one can't hear oneself speak — and they don't seem to have any rules in particular; at least, if there are, nobody attends to them — and you've no idea how confusing it is all the things being alive; for instance, there's the arch I've got to go through next walking about at the other end of the ground — and I should have croqueted the Queen's hedgehog just now, only it ran away when it saw mine coming!"

"How do you like the Queen?" said the Cat in a low voice.

"Not at all," said Alice; "she's so extremely —" Just then she noticed that the Queen was close behind her listening: so she went on, "— likely to win, that it's hardly worth while finishing the game."

The Queen smiled and passed on.

"Who *are* you talking to?" said the King, coming up to Alice, and looking at the Cat's head with great curiosity.

"It's a friend of mine — a Cheshire Cat," said Alice; "allow me to introduce it."

"I don't like the look of it at all," said the King; "however, it may kiss my hand if it likes."

"I'd rather not," the Cat remarked.

"Don't be impertinent," said the King, "and don't look at me like that!" He got behind Alice as he spoke.

"A cat may look at a king," said Alice. "I've read that in some book, but I don't remember where."

29

"Well, it must be removed," said the King very decidedly, and he called to the Queen, who was passing at the moment, "My dear! I wish you would have this cat removed!"

The Queen had only one way of settling all difficulties, great or small. "Off with his head!" she said, without even looking around.

"I'll fetch the executioner myself," said the King eagerly, and he hurried off.

Alice thought she might as well go back and see how the game was going on, as she heard the Queen's voice in the distance, screaming with passion. She had already heard her sentence of three of the players to be executed for having missed their turns, and she did not like the look of things at all, as the game was in such confusion that she never knew whether it was her turn or not. So she went in search of her hedgehog.

The hedgehog was engaged in a fight with another hedgehog, which seemed to Alice an excellent opportunity for croqueting one of them with the other: the only difficulty was, that her flamingo was gone across to the other side of the garden, where Alice could see it trying in a helpless sort of way to fly up into one of the trees.

By the time she had caught the flamingo and brought it back, the fight was over, and both the hedgehogs were out of sight: "but it doesn't matter much," thought Alice, "as all the arches are gone from this side of the ground." So she tucked it under her arm, that it might not escape again, and went back for a little more conversation with her friend.

When she got back to the Cheshire Cat, she was surprised to find quite a large crowd collected around it: there was a dispute going on between the executioner, the King, and the Queen, who were all talking at once, while all the rest were quite silent, and looked very uncomfortable.

The moment Alice appeared, she was appealed to by all three to settle the question, and they repeated their arguments to her, though, as they all spoke at once, she found it very hard to make out exactly what they said.

The executioner's argument was, that you couldn't cut off a head unless there was a body to

cut it off from; that he had never had to do such a thing before, and he wasn't going to begin at *his* time of life.

The King's argument was, that anything that had a head could be beheaded, and that you weren't to talk nonsense.

The Queen's argument was, that if something wasn't done about it in less than no time, she'd have everybody executed, all round. (It was this last remark that had made the whole party look so grave and anxious.)

Alice could think of nothing else to say but, "It belongs to the Duchess: you'd better ask *her* about it."

"She's in prison," the Queen said to the executioner; "fetch her here." And the executioner went off like an arrow.

The Cat's head began fading away the moment he was gone, and, by the time he had come back with the Duchess, it had entirely disappeared.

WHO IS TO BLAME?

My uncle, Pyotr Demyanych, a skinny, bilious collegiate assessor very much resembling a stale smoked salmon with a stick struck through it, was getting ready to go to the high school where he taught Latin, when he noticed that the binding of his grammar book had been nibbled by mice.

"I say there, Praskovya," he said, going into the kitchen and addressing the cook. "How do we happen to have mice around here? For heaven's sake! Yesterday they chewed holes in my top hat, and now they've desecrated my grammar book. The next thing you know, they'll start eating my clothes!"

"What am I supposed to do about it?" answered Praskovya. "I didn't bring them into the house."

"*Something* has to be done! You could get us a cat, couldn't you?"

CHEKHOV

"We already have one, but what's he good for?" And Praskovya pointed to a corner, where a white kitten, thin as a sliver, was curled up asleep beside a twig broom.

"Why isn't he good for anything?" asked Pyotr Demyanych.

"He's still young and stupid. He can't be as much as two months old yet."

"Hm... Then he should be taught. It would be better for him to be learning than just lying there."

Having said that, Pyotr Demyanych sighed a care-worn sigh and walked out of the kitchen. The kitten raised his head lazily, watched him leave, and again closed his eyes.

The kitten was awake, though, and thinking. About what? Being unfamiliar with real life, and having no store of impressions, he could think only instinctually, and envision life only according to those notions he had inherited, together with his flesh and blood, from his tiger ancestors. (*Vide* Darwin.) His thoughts were on the order of daydreams. His feline imagination pictured something like the Arabian desert, across which moved shadows very much resembling Praskovya, the stove, the broom. Among the shadows there suddenly appeared a saucer of milk. The saucer grew paws, and began to move and manifest an inclination to flee. The kitten pounced and, in a swoon of bloodthirsty voluptuousness, sank his claws into it.... When the saucer had vanished into the mist, a piece of meat appeared, dropped by Praskovya. With a cowardly squeak, the meat started to run away; but the kitten pounced, and sank his claws into it.... Each one of the young daydreamer's visions had as its starting point pounces, claws, and teeth....

The soul of another is a mystery, and a cat's soul even more so. Nonetheless, just how close the foregoing images are to the truth, is evident from the following incident. Under the spell of his daydreams, the kitten suddenly gave a start, looked with glittering eyes at Praskovya and, his fur bristling, pounced, sinking his claws into the hem of her skirt. Obviously he was a born mouser, fully worthy of his bloodthirsty ancestors. Fate had intended him to be the terror of cellars, pantries, and granaries. And had it not been for education.... But let us

not get ahead of the story.

On his way home from the school, Pyotr Demyanych went into a variety store and bought a mousetrap for fifteen kopecks. After dinner he put a piece of chopped meat on the hook and placed the trap under the sofa, where there was a pile of students' assignment papers that Praskovya used for household purposes. Exactly at six o'clock in the evening, when the venerable Latinist was sitting at his desk and correcting papers, a sudden *clunk!* came from under the sofa — so loud that my uncle started and dropped his pen. Without delay, he went to the sofa and retrieved the trap. A neat little mouse about the size of a thimble was sniffing the wire of the cage and trembling with fright.

"Aha!" muttered Pyotr Demyanych. And he glared so balefully at the mouse that you'd have thought he was about to give him an "F." "You're caught, you vile creature! Just you wait! I'll show you how to eat grammar books!"

Having had his fill of glaring at his victim, Pyotr Demyanych put the mousetrap on the floor and shouted, "Praskovya! I've caught a mouse! Brink the kitten here!"

"R-r-right away!" Praskovya called back. And a moment later she came in, holding in her arms the descendant of tigers.

"Fine!" muttered Pyotr Demyanych, rubbing his hands. "We're going to teach him. Put him down by the mousetrap.... That's it.... Let him smell it and look at it.... That's the way...."

The kitten looked with astonishment at my uncle, then at his armchair; sniffed the mousetrap with a baffled air; and then — no doubt having been frightened by the bright lamplight and all the attention being paid to him — took off in terror toward the door.

"Stop!" shouted my uncle, seizing him by the tail. "Stop, you scoundrel! You've been frightened by a *mouse*, you idiot! Look: it's a mouse. Come, look! Well? *Look*, I tell you!"

Pyotr Demyanych grabbed the kitten by the scruff of the neck and shoved his nose against the mousetrap.

"Look, you little bastard! Pick him up, Praskovya, and hold him.... Hold him against the door of the trap.... When I let the mouse out, you let him go at the same time, understand? Let him go at exactly the same time. All right?"

My uncle assumed a conspiratorial expression and raised the door.... The mouse emerged hesitantly, sniffed the air and then darted under the sofa. The liberated kitten hoisted his tail in the air, and ran under the desk.

"It got away! It got away!" shouted Pyotr Demyanych, making a ferocious face. "Where is he, the villain? Under the desk? Just you wait...."

My uncle dragged the kitten out from under the desk and shook him in the air....

"You scum!" he muttered, pulling him by the ear. "Take that! And that! Will you ever flunk like that again? You s-s-scum!"

The next day, Praskovya once again heard the shout: "Praskovya, I've caught a mouse! Bring the kitten here!"

After his humiliation of the day before, the kitten had gone to hide under the stove, and had not come out all night. When Praskovya had dragged him out and, carrying him by the scruff of the neck into the study, had deposited him in front of the mousetrap, he trembled all over and meowed plaintively.

"All right," Pyotr Demyanych commanded. "Let him get the lay of the land first. Let him look and sniff. Look and learn, you! Stop, damn you!" he shouted, noticing that the kitten was backing away from the mousetrap. "I'll thrash you! Hold on to him by the ear. That's it.... Now put him down in front of the door."

My uncle slowly raised the door.... The mouse whisked right under the kitten's nose, ricocheted off Praskovya's arm, and ran under the bookcase. The kitten, meanwhile, sensing that he was at liberty, made a desperate leap and hid under the sofa.

"He's let another mouse go!" bellowed Pyotr Demyanych. "Do you call that a cat? He's an abomination! Just plain trash! He needs to be thrashed — thrashed right in front of the mousetrap!"

37

CHEKHOV

When the third mouse was caught, the kitten trembled all over at the sight of the mouse-trap and its tenant, and scratched Praskovya's hand.... After the fourth mouse, my uncle lost all self-control and gave the kitten a kick. "Get rid of this nasty thing!" he said. "I want him out of the house today! Just dump him somewhere. He isn't worth a tinker's damn!"

A year went by. The thin, sickly kitten developed into a solid, sagacious tomcat. One night he was prowling through the backyards on his way to a lovers' tryst. He was already near his destination when suddenly he heard a rustling sound, then saw a mouse scampering from the horse-trough toward the stables.... Our hero bristled, arched his back, began to hiss and, shaking all over, pusillanimously took to flight.

Alas! Sometimes I feel that I'm in the ludicrous position of the fleeing tomcat. Like the kitten, I had the honor in my time of studying Latin with my uncle. Today, whenever I chance to see some work of classical antiquity, instead of going into wild raptures about it I begin to recall the *ut consecutivum*, the irregular verbs, the sallow-gray face of my uncle, and the ablative absolute.... I go pale, my hair stands on end, and like the tomcat, I take off in ignominious flight.

THE LONG-CAT

A short-haired black cat always looks longer than any other cat. But this particular one, Babou, nick-named the Long-cat, really did measure, stretched right out flat, well over a yard and a quarter. If you did not arrange him properly, he was not much more than a yard. I used to measure him sometimes.

"He's stopped growing longer," I said one day to my mother. "Isn't it a pity?"

"Why a pity? He's too long as it is. I can't understand why you want everything to grow bigger. It's bad to grow too much, very bad indeed!"

It's true that it always worried her when she thought that children were growing too fast, and she had good cause to be anxious about my elder half-brother, who went on growing until he was twenty-four.

"But I'd love to grow a bit taller."

"D'you mean you'd like to be like that

COLETTE

39

Brisedoux girl, five-foot-seven tall at twelve years old? A midget can always make herself liked. But what can you do with a gigantic beauty? Who would want to marry her?"

"Couldn't Babou get married, then?"

"Oh, a cat's a cat. Babou's only too long when he really wants to be. Are we even sure he's black? He's probably white in snowy weather, dark blue at night, and red when he goes to steal strawberries. He's very light when he lies on your knees, and very heavy when I carry him into the kitchen in the evenings to prevent him from sleeping on my bed. I think he's too much of a vegetarian to be a real cat."

For the Long-cat really did steal strawberries, picking out the ripest of the variety called Docteur-Morère which are so sweet, and of the white Hautboys which taste faintly of ants. According to the season he would also go for the tender tips of the asparagus, and when it came to melons his choice was not so much for cantaloupes as for the kind called Noir-des-Carmes whose rind, marbled light and dark like the skin of a salamander, he knew how to rip open. In all this he was not at all exceptional. I once had a she-cat who used to crunch rings of raw onion, provided they were the sweet onions of the South. There are cats who set great store by oysters, snails, and clams.

When the Long-cat went off to poach strawberries from our next-door neighbor, Monsieur Pomié, he went by way of the wall, which was covered with such dense ivy that the cats could walk along under cover, their presence revealed only by the quivering of the leaves, the mist of yellow pollen and the golden cloud of bees.

He loved his leafy tunnel but, do what he would, he had to come out of it at the end since Madame Pomié kept the top of the wall bare where it overlooked her garden. Once out in the open, he adopted a very off-hand manner, especially if he met Madame de Saint-Aubin's beautiful cat, who was black, with a white face and belly. I found this wall a good place to study tomcats, not so much their habits as their ceremonial procedure, governed by a kind of choreography. Unlike the females, they are more noisy than warlike and they try to gain time by

palavers. Hence all the snarling preambles. Not that they do not know how to fight cruelly once they come to grips; but as a rule they are far removed from the silent and furious grapplings of the females. The she-cat we had at the same time as the Long-cat literally flew into battle if a female ventured into her haunts. Barely touching the ground, she would pounce on the enemy, even if it were her own offspring. She fought as a bird does, going for her adversary's head. I never saw her chastise a male, except for a few cuffs, for as soon as the males saw her they fled, while she followed them with a look of inexpressible contempt. When July and January came, she settled her amorous encounters in forty-eight hours. On the morning of the third day, when the chosen partner, in fine fettle and with renewed appetite, approached her with a self-confident, prancing gait and a deep-throated song, she would root him to the spot with a mere look.

"I've come," he would begin, "I... I came to resume our agreeable conversation of yesterday..."

"Excuse me," the she-cat interrupted, "you were saying? I didn't quite catch. What agreeable conversation?"

"Why... the one we had at ten o'clock in the morning... and the one at five in the afternoon... and especially our conversation at ten in the evening, near the well."

The she-cat, perched on top of the pergola, raised herself a little on her delicately-boned paws.

"Near the well, a conversation, you, with ME? Who do you suppose is going to believe that? You don't expect ME to! Take yourself off! It'll be the worse for you if you don't, I can tell you. Take yourself off!"

"But... but I love you. And I'm ready to prove it to you again."

Standing upright there the she-cat towered over the tom as Satan, jutting out from Notre Dame, broods over Paris. The look she cast on him from her tawny-gold eyes was such as he could not long endure; and the outcast would make off with the shambling gait of someone who has been driven away.

As I was saying then, the Long-cat, impelled by a vegetarian craving which those who have not experienced it can never understand, would go after the strawberries, the melons and the asparagus. On his return, a little green or rosy pulp remained, as evidence of his pillagings, in the grooves between his curved claws, and this he licked casually during his siesta.

"Show your hands!" my mother used to say to him, and thereupon he surrendered to her a long front paw, adept at every kind of mischief, with pads as hard as a road parched with drought.

"Have you been opening a melon?"

I dare say he understood. His gentle yellow eyes met Sido's penetrating look, but since his innocence was only assumed, he could not help squinting a little.

"Yes, you *have* opened a melon. And I expect it was the pretty little one I had my eye on, the one that looked like a globe with yellow continents and green seas." She released the long paw which fell back limp and expressionless.

"That deserves a good slap," said I.

"I know. But just think that instead of a melon he might have slit open a bird, or a little rabbit, or have eaten a chick."

She scratched the flat skull which he stretched up against her hand, and the half-bald temples which showed bluish between the sparse black hairs. A tremendous purring rose from his thick neck with its white patch under the chin. The Long-cat loved no one but my mother, followed no one but her and looked to her for everything. If I took him in my arms he would imperceptibly glide out of them as though he were melting away. Except for the ritual battles and during the brief seasons of love-making, the Long-cat was nothing but silence, sleep and nonchalant night-prowlings.

I naturally preferred our she-cats to him. The females of the feline tribe are so unlike the males that they seem to regard the tom as a stranger and often as an enemy. The only excep-

tions are the cats of Siam who live in couples like the wild beasts. Perhaps it is because the cats in our countries are such a hybrid collection of every coat and color that they develop a taste for change and fickleness. In my home we were never without two or three she-cats who graced the lawns, crowned the pump and slept in the wisteria, which they had hollowed into a hammock. They confined their charming sociability to my mother and myself. As soon as January and July, the compulsory seasons of love, were over, they regarded the male once again as a suspect, a lout, and a wicked devourer of newly-born kittens, and their conversations with the Long-cat consisted chiefly of crisp insults, whenever he assumed the bland, gentle manner and the innocent smile of the cat who has never harbored any evil intentions, or even thoughts. Sometimes they seemed about to play, but this never came to anything. The females took fright at the strength of the male, and at that furious excitement which, in an uncastrated cat, turns playfulness into a murderous combat.

By virtue of his serpent-like build, the Long-cat excelled at strange leaps in which he nearly twisted himself into a figure of eight. In full sunlight his winter coat, which was longer and more satiny than in summer, revealed the waterings and markings of his far-off tabby ancestor. A tom will remain playful until he is quite old; but even in play his face never loses the gravity that is stamped on it. The Long-cat's expression softened only when he looked at my mother. Then his white whiskers would bristle powerfully, while into his eyes crept the smile of an innocent little boy. He used to follow her when she went to pick violets along the wall that separated M. de Fourolles' garden from ours. The close-set border provided every day a big bunch which my mother let fade, either pinned to her bodice or in an empty glass, because violets in water lose all their scent. Step by step the Long-cat followed his stooping mistress, sometimes imitating with his paw the gesture of her hand groping among the leaves, and imitating her discoveries also. "Ha, ha!" he would cry, "me too!" and thereupon show his prize: a bombardier beetle, a pink worm or a shriveled cockchafer.

"My goodness, how silly you are," Sido would say to him, affectionately. "Never mind,

what you've found is very pretty."

When we rejoined my elder brother in the Loiret, we took with us our favorite she-cat and the Long-cat. Both of them seemed to mind much less than I did exchanging a lovely house for a small cottage, and the vast grounds of our family property for a narrow garden. I have referred elsewhere to the stream which danced at the end of this garden. Left to itself, it was sufficiently clear and sparkling, and had enough soap-wort and wild radishes clinging to the walls which hemmed it in, to beautify any village, if the village had respected it. But those who lived on its banks polluted it.

At the end of our new garden there was a little wash-house which protected the straw palli-asse on which the washerwomen knelt, the sloping board, white as a scraped bone, where they pressed the frothing linen, the washerwomen's battledores, the brushes made of couch-grass and the sprinklers. Soon after our arrival the she-cat laid claim to the palliasse, gave birth to her litter on it, and brought up there the one little tabby which we left her. Whenever the sun shone I joined her there and sat on the soaping-board. The tabby kitten, soft and heavy with milk, watched the reflections of the little river forming broken rings, gold serpents and wave-lets on the tiled roof of the penthouse. At six weeks he was already trotting, and following the flight of the flies with eyes that were still blue, while his mother, with a coat as finely marked as his, saw herself mirrored in the beauty of her son.

Excluded though he was from this family happiness, the Long-cat for all that adopted an air of serenity that was vaguely patriarchal, the detached bearing of those fathers who are con-tent to leave the care of their offspring to their worthy spouse. He confined himself to the parsley bed which the she-cat let him have, and there he would sprawl, warming his long belly, with its withered teats, in the sun. Or else he would drape himself over the heap of fire-wood, as if the spiky faggots were wool and down. For a cat's idea of what is comfortable and what is not is incomprehensible to a human.

Spring drenched our retreat with precocious warmth, and in the light air of May the scents

of lilac, young tarragon and red-brown wallflower intermingled. I was at that time a prey to homesickness for my native village, and this I nursed in silence in the new village, amidst the bitterness of spring and its first flowers. There I sat, an anemic young girl, leaning my cheeks and my little waxen ears against a wall already warm, the end of one of my over-long plaits always trailing far from me over the fine, sieved leaf-mold of a seed-bed.

One day when we were all dozing, the she-cat on her palliasse, the tom on his couch of spiky firewood-bundles, and I at the foot of the wall where the sun lingered longest, the little cat, who was wide awake and busy chasing flies on the edge of the river, fell into the water. True to the code of his tribe, he uttered no cry and began to swim by instinct as soon as he came to the surface. I happened to see him tumble in, and just as I was setting off for the house to seize the butterfly net, run down the road, and rejoin the river at the first little bridge, where I could have fished out the swimming kitten, the Long-cat threw himself into the water. He swam like an otter, ears flat and only his nostrils out of the water.

It is not every day that one sees a cat swim, swim of his own free will, I mean. He can glide unerringly through the water like a serpent, but he never makes use of this gift except to save his life if he is in danger of drowning. Helped by the current, the Long-cat forged ahead strongly in pursuit of the kitten, the swift, transparent water of the pent-up river on its bed of pebbles and broken shards making his long body look like a leech. I lost half a minute through stopping to watch him.

He seized the little cat by the scruff of its neck, turned right round and set off upstream, not without effort, for the current was strong and the kitten, inert like all little cats when you hold them by the scruff of their necks, weighed his full weight. The sight of the Long-cat struggling nearly made me jump into the water too. But the rescuer clambered on to the washing-board and laid his dripping burden on the bank, after which he shook himself and looked in stupefaction at the drenching kitten. That was the moment when the rescued one, silent hitherto, elected to cough and sneeze and set up a terrific shrill lamentation which awoke the mother cat.

"Horrors!" she cried. "What do I see? You baby-snatcher! You wrecker, you devourer of infants, you stinking beast, what have you done to my son?"

Even as she jerked out these insults at the top of her voice, she was already encircling the little cat with her own body and sniffing him, finding time to turn him all over and lick the river water off his coat.

"But," ventured the Long-cat, "but... but on the contrary, I jumped into the water to get him. Now I come to think of it, I don't know what made me do it!"

"Out of my sight! Or in another moment I'll bite your nose off and crush the breath out of you! I'll blind you, I'll slit your throat, I'll..."

She made ready to suit the action to the word, and I admired the furious beauty which animates a female when she pits herself against danger or an adversary bigger than herself.

The Long-cat took to his heels and, still dripping, gained the ladder leading to the cozy hay-loft warm under its tiled roof. The she-cat, changing her tone, led her son to the palliasse where he found once again the warm maternal belly with its milk, healing care and restoring sleep.

But the she-cat never forgave the Long-cat. Whenever she met him she never forgot to call him "baby-snatcher, drowner of little cats, assassin," accompanying this with snarls and yells, while the Long-cat strove each time to clear himself: "Now look here! I tell you that, on the contrary, it was I who, obeying only my own heart, overcame my loathing for cold water..."

I genuinely pitied him and used to call him "poor, misunderstood Long-cat."

"Misunderstood," said my mother, "that remains to be seen."

She could see deep into souls; and she was not one to be taken in by the equivocal meekness, the flickering yellow gleam in the eye of a tomcat, whenever it lights on tender, defenseless flesh.

A PERSIAN TALE

"Have you ever," I said to Jim, looking up from my book, "have you ever heard of Rustem?"

Jim looked at me scornfully; his whiskers twitched in the firelight. "Of Rustem," he said, "our great Persian Hero? What do you think?" He blinked his yellow eyes thoughtfully. "I'll tell you a story about him that you won't find in any of your books," he said.

And this is the story:

Once Rustem, who was a brave fighter, saved a magician from some robbers who had fallen upon him suddenly in a lonely place. Rustem invited the old man to spend the night in his tent, and after supper they sat outside in the cool air and watched a big fire which Rustem's servants had lighted. It was a clear, starlight night, but there was a quick little breeze fluttering about.

It caught the smoke of the fire so that it

FYLEMAN

danced and whirled about in a thousand queer shapes. The stars seemed to dance with the smoke, they glittered and gleamed between the eddies, and here and there a little tongue of darting flame joined in the dance too. Presently the magician spoke.

"I should like to make thee a gift, Rustem," he said, "in return for what thou hast done for me. What beautiful thing dost thou desire?"

"I desire nothing," said Rustem. "What could be more beautiful than that smoke and the fire and the stars?"

"I will make a gift for thee out of the smoke and the flame and the stars," said the magician.

And he took a handful of smoke and a flame of fire and two bright stars, and kneaded them together for a minute.

"There," he said, "there is thy gift."

Rustem was delighted, for the magician had made a little live creature, soft and grey like the smoke, with bright, star-like eyes and with a little red tongue like a tiny flame of fire. It danced and capered about, and was a joy to look upon.

"Take it home," said the magician. "It will be a plaything for thy children and an ornament to thy house."

And Rustem did so.

* * *

"And that," said Jim, "is how the first Persian kitten came into the world. And I ought to know. It was my earliest ancestor."

50

PUSS IN BOOTS

There was a miller who left no more estate to the three sons he had than his mill, his ass, and his cat. The partition was soon made. Neither scrivener nor attorney was sent for. They would soon have eaten up all the poor patrimony. The eldest had the mill, the second the ass, and the youngest nothing but the cat. The poor young fellow was quite comfortless at having so poor a lot.

"My brothers," said he, "may get their living handsomely enough by joining their stocks together; but for my part, when I have eaten up my cat and made me a muff of his skin, I must die of hunger."

The cat, who heard all this, but made as if he did not, said to him with a grave and serious air:

"Do not thus afflict yourself, my good master. Your fortunes are not so bad as you seem to think. You do not value me highly

PERRAULT

enough. You need only give me a bag and get a pair of boots made for me that I may scamper through the dirt and the brambles, and you shall see that you have not so bad a portion of me as you imagine."

The cat's master did not build very much upon what he said. He had often seen him play a great many cunning tricks to catch rats and mice, as when he used to hang by the heels, or hide himself in the meal, and make as if he were dead; so that he did not altogether despair of his affording him some help in his miserable condition. When the cat had what he asked for, he booted himself very gallantly, and putting his bag about his neck, he held the strings of it in his two fore paws and went into a warren where there was a great abundance of rabbits. He put bran and sow-thistle into his bag, and stretching out at length, as if he had been dead, he waited for some young rabbits, not yet acquainted with the deceits of the world, to come and rummage his bag for what he had put into it.

Scarce was he lain down but he had what he wanted. Two rash and foolish young rabbits jumped into his bag, and Monsieur Puss, immediately drawing close the strings, took them away without pity. Proud of his prey, he went with it to the palace and asked to speak with his majesty. He was shown upstairs into the King's apartment, and making a low reverence, said to him:

"I have brought you, sire, two rabbits of the warren, which my noble lord the Marquis of Carabas (for that was the title which Puss was pleased to give his master) has commanded me to present to your majesty from him."

"Tell your master," said the King, "that I thank him and that he does me a great deal of pleasure."

Another time he went and hid himself among some standing corn, holding still his bag open, and when a brace of partridges ran into it, he drew the strings and so caught them both. He went and made a present of these to the King, as he had done before of the rabbits which he took in the warren. The King, in like manner, received the partridges with great pleasure and

ordered him some money for drink.

The cat continued for two or three months thus to carry his majesty, from time to time, game of his master's taking. One day in particular, when he knew for certain that he was to take the air along the riverside with his daughter, the most beautiful princess in the world, he said to his master:

"If you will follow my advice your fortune is made. You need only go and wash yourself in the river, in that part I shall show you, and leave the rest to me."

The Marquis of Carabas did what the cat advised him to, without knowing why or where-fore. While he was washing the King passed by, and the cat began to cry out:

"Help! help! My Lord Marquis of Carabas is going to be drowned."

At this noise the King put his head out of the coach-window, finding it was the cat who had so often brought him such good game, he commanded his guards to run immediately to the assistance of his lordship the Marquis of Carabas. While they were drawing the poor mar-quis out of the river, the cat came up to the coach and told the King that while his master was washing there came by some rogues, who went off with his clothes, though he had cried out "Thieves! thieves!" several times as loud as he could.

This cunning cat had hidden them under a great stone. The King immediately commanded the officers of his wardrobe to run and fetch one of his best suits for the Marquis of Carabas.

The King caressed him after a very extraordinary manner, and as the fine clothes he had given him extremely set off his good mien (for he was well-built and very handsome in his person), the King's daughter took a secret inclination to him, and the Marquis of Carabas had no sooner cast two or three respectful and somewhat tender glances but she fell in love with him to distraction. The King would needs have him come into the coach and take part of the airing. The cat, quite overjoyed to see his project begin to succeed, marched on before, and meeting with some countrymen who were mowing a meadow, he said to them:

"Good people, you who are mowing, if you do not tell the King that the meadow you mow belongs to my Lord Marquis of Carabas, you shall be chopped as fine as herbs for the pot."

The King did not fail to ask of the mowers to whom the meadow they were mowing belonged.

"To my Lord Marquis of Carabas," they answered all together, for the cat's threats had made them terribly afraid.

"This," said the marquis, "is a meadow which never fails to yield a plentiful harvest every year."

The master cat, who went still on before, met with some reapers and said to them:

"Good people, you who are reaping, if you do not tell the King that all this corn belongs to the Marquis of Carabas, you shall be chopped as fine as herbs for the pot."

The King, who passed by a moment after, would needs know to whom all that corn did belong.

"To my Lord Marquis of Carabas," replied the reapers, and the King was very well pleased with it, as well as with the marquis, whom he congratulated thereupon. The master cat, who went always before, said the same words to all he met, and the King was astonished at the vast estates of my Lord Marquis of Carabas. Lord Monsieur Puss came at last to a stately castle, the master of which was an ogre, the richest that had ever been known; for all the lands which the king had then gone over belonged to this castle. The cat, who had taken care to inform himself who this ogre was and what he could do, asked to speak with him, saying he could not pass so near his castle without having the honor of paying his respects to him.

The ogre admitted him and made him sit down.

"I have been assured," said the cat, "that you have the gift of being able to change yourself into all sorts of creatures you have a mind to. You can, for example, transform yourself into a lion, or an elephant."

"That is true," answered the ogre very briskly; "and to convince you, you shall see me now become a lion."

Puss was so sadly terrified at the sight of a lion so near him that he cried out loudly, and would have run away had not the ogre quickly resumed his natural form. However, he owned he had been very much frightened.

"I have been moreover informed," said the cat, "but I know not how to believe it, that you have also the power to take on you the shape of the smallest animals; for example, to change yourself into a rat or a mouse. But I must own to you I take this to be impossible."

"Impossible!" cried the ogre. "You shall see that presently."

And at the same time he changed himself into a mouse and began to run about the floor. Puss no sooner perceived this but he fell upon him and ate him up.

Meanwhile the King, who saw, as he passed, this fine castle of the ogre's, noted its beauty and marveled at its size and grandeur. He had a mind to go into it, and ordered his coach to be driven up to the entrance. Puss, who heard the noise of his majesty's coach running over the drawbridge, ran out and said to the King:

"Your majesty is welcome to this castle of my Lord Marquis of Carabas."

"What! my Lord Marquis," cried the King, "and does this castle also belong to you? There can be nothing finer than this court and all the stately buildings which surround it. Let us go into it, if you please."

The marquis gave his hand to the princess and followed the King, who went first. They passed into a spacious hall, where they found a magnificent collation, which the ogre had prepared for his friends who were that very day to visit him but dared not enter, knowing the King was there. His majesty was perfectly charmed with the good qualities of my Lord Marquis of Carabas, as was his daughter, who had fallen violently in love with him, and seeing the vast estate he possessed, said to him, after having drunk five or six glasses:

"It will be owing to yourself only, my Lord Marquis, if you are not my son-in-law."

The marquis, making several low bows, accepted the honor which his majesty conferred upon him, and forthwith that very same day, married the princess.

Puss became a great lord and never ran after mice any more but only for his diversion.

TOBERMORY

It was a chill, rain-washed afternoon of a late August day, that indefinite season when partridges are still in security or cold storage, and there is nothing to hunt — unless one is bounded on the north by the Bristol Channel, in which case one may lawfully gallop after fat red stags. Lady Blemley's house party was not bounded on the north by the Bristol Channel, hence there was a full gathering of her guests round the tea table on this particular afternoon. And, in spite of the blankness of the season and the triteness of the occasion, there was no trace in the company of that fatigued restlessness which means a dread of the pianola and a subdued hankering for auction bridge. The undisguised openmouthed attention of the entire party was fixed on the homely negative personality of Mr. Cornelius Appin. Of all her guests, he was the one who had come to

Lady Blemley with the vaguest reputation. Someone had said he was "clever," and he had gotten his invitation in the moderate expectation, on the part of his hostess, that some portion at least of his cleverness would be contributed to the general entertainment. Until teatime that day she had been unable to discover in what direction, if any, his cleverness lay. He was neither a wit nor a croquet champion, a hypnotic force nor a begetter of amateur theatricals. Neither did his exterior suggest the sort of man in whom women are willing to pardon a generous measure of mental deficiency. He had subsided into mere Mr. Appin, and the Cornelius seemed a piece of transparent baptismal bluff. And now he was claiming to have launched on the world a discovery beside which the invention of gun powder, of the printing press, and of steam locomotion were inconsiderable trifles. Science had made bewildering strides in many directions during recent decades, but this thing seemed to belong to the domain of miracle rather than to scientific achievement.

"And do you really ask us to believe," Sir Wilfrid was saying, "that you have discovered a means for instructing animals in the art of human speech, and that dear old Tobermory has proved your first successful pupil?"

"It is a problem at which I have worked for the last seventeen years," said Mr. Appin, "but only during the last eight or nine months have I been rewarded with glimmerings of success. Of course I have experimented with thousands of animals, but latterly only with cats, those wonderful creatures which have assimilated themselves so marvelously with our civilization while retaining all their highly developed feral instincts. Here and there among cats one comes across an outstanding superior intellect, just as one does among the ruck of human beings, and when I made the acquaintance of Tobermory a week ago I saw at once that I was in contact with a 'Beyond-cat' of extraordinary intelligence. I had gone far along the road to success in recent experiments; with Tobermory, as you call him, I have reached the goal."

Mr. Appin concluded his remarkable statement in a voice which he strove to divest of a triumphant inflection. No one said "Rats," though Clovis's lips moved in a monosyllabic

58

contortion which probably invoked those rodents of disbelief.

"And do you mean to say," asked Miss Resker, after a slight pause, "that you have taught Tobermory to say and understand easy sentences of one syllable?"

"My dear Miss Resker," said the wonder-worker patiently, "one teaches little children and savages and backward adults in that piecemeal fashion; when one has once solved the problem of making a beginning with an animal of highly developed intelligence one has no need for those halting methods. Tobermory can speak our language with perfect correctness."

This time Clovis very distinctly said, "Beyond-rats!" Sir Wilfrid was more polite, but equally skeptical.

"Hadn't we better have the cat in and judge for ourselves?" suggested Lady Blemley.

Sir Wilfrid went in search of the animal, and the company settled themselves down to the languid expectation of witnessing some more or less adroit drawing-room ventriloquism.

In a minute Sir Wilfrid was back in the room, his face white beneath its tan and his eyes dilated with excitement.

"By Gad, it's true!"

His agitation was unmistakably genuine, and his hearers started forward in a thrill of awakened interest.

Collapsing into an armchair he continued breathlessly: "I found him dozing in the smoking room, and called out to him to come for his tea. He blinked at me in his usual way, and I said, 'Come on, Toby; don't keep us waiting;' and, by Gad! he drawled out in a most horribly natural voice that he'd come when he dashed well pleased! I nearly jumped out of my skin!"

Appin had preached to absolutely incredulous hearers; Sir Wilfrid's statement carried instant conviction. A Babel-like chorus of startled exclamation arose, amid which the scientist sat mutely enjoying the first fruit of his stupendous discovery.

In the midst of the clamor Tobermory entered the room and made his way with velvet tread and studied unconcern across to the group seated round the tea table.

A sudden hush of awkwardness and constraint fell on the company. Somehow there seemed an element of embarrassment in addressing on equal terms a domestic cat of acknowledged dental ability.

"Will you have some milk, Tobermory?" asked Lady Blemley in a rather strained voice.

"I don't mind if I do," was the response, couched in a tone of even indifference. A shiver of suppressed excitement went through the listeners, and Lady Blemley might be excused for pouring out the saucerful of milk rather unsteadily.

"I'm afraid I've spilled a good deal of it," she said apologetically.

"After all, it's not my Axminster," was Tobermory's rejoinder.

Another silence fell on the group, and then Miss Resker, in her best district-visitor manner, asked if the human language had been difficult to learn. Tobermory looked squarely at her for a moment and then fixed his gaze serenely on the middle distance. It was obvious that boring questions lay outside his scheme of life.

"What do you think of human intelligence?" asked Mavis Pellington lamely.

"Of whose intelligence in particular?" asked Tobermory coldly.

"Oh, well, mine for instance," said Mavis, with a feeble laugh.

"You put me in an embarrassing position," said Tobermory, whose tone and attitude certainly did not suggest a shred of embarrassment. "When your inclusion in this house party was suggested Sir Wilfrid protested that you were the most brainless woman of his acquaintance, and that there was a wide distinction between hospitality and care of the feebleminded. Lady Blemley replied that your lack of brain power was the precise quality which had earned you your invitation, as you were the only person she could think of who might be idiotic enough to buy their old car. You know, the one they call 'The Envy of Sisyphus,' because it goes quite nicely uphill if you push it."

Lady Blemley's protestations would have had greater effect if she had not casually suggested to Mavis only that morning that the car in question would be just the thing for her down at her Devonshire home.

Major Barfield plunged in heavily to effect a diversion.

"How about your carryings-on with the tortoiseshell puss up at the stables, eh?"

The moment he had said it everyone realized the blunder.

"One does not usually discuss these matters in public," said Tobermory frigidly. "From a slight observation of your ways since you've been in this house I should imagine you'd find it inconvenient if I were to shift the conversation on to your own little affairs."

The panic which ensued was not confined to the major.

"Would you like to go and see if cook has got your dinner ready?" suggested Lady Blemley hurriedly, affecting to ignore the fact that it wanted at least two hours to Tobermory's dinnertime.

"Thanks," said Tobermory, "not quite so soon after my tea. I don't want to die of indigestion."

"Cats have nine lives, you know," said Sir Wilfrid heartily.

"Possibly," answered Tobermory; "but only one liver."

"Adelaide!" said Mrs. Cornett, "do you mean to encourage that cat to go out and gossip about us in the servants' hall?"

The panic had indeed become general. A narrow ornamental balustrade ran in front of most of the bedroom windows at the Towers, and it was recalled with dismay that this had formed a favorite promenade for Tobermory at all hours, whence he could watch the pigeons — and heaven knew what else besides. If he intended to become reminiscent in his present outspoken strain, the effect would be something more than disconcerting. Mrs. Cornett, who spent much time at her toilet table, and whose complexion was reputed to be of a nomadic though punctual disposition, looked as ill at ease as the major. Miss Scrawen, who wrote fiercely sensuous poetry and led a blameless life, merely displayed irritation; if you are methodical and virtuous in private you don't necessarily want everyone to know it. Bertie van Tahn, who was

so depraved at seventeen that he had long ago given up trying to be any worse, turned a dull shade of gardenia white, but he did not commit the error of dashing out of the room like Odo Finsberry, a young gentleman who was understood to be reading for the Church and who was possibly disturbed at the thought of scandals he might hear concerning other people. Clovis had the presence of mind to maintain a composed exterior; privately he was calculating how long it would take to procure a box of fancy mice through the agency of the Exchange and Mart as a species of hush money.

Even in a delicate situation like the present, Agnes Resker could not endure to remain too long in the background.

"Why did I ever come down here?" she asked dramatically.

Tobermory immediately accepted the opening.

"Judging by what you said to Mrs. Cornett on the croquet lawn yesterday, you were out for food. You described the Blemleys as the dullest people to stay with that you knew, but said they were clever enough to employ a first-rate cook; otherwise they'd find it difficult to get anyone to come down a second time."

"There's not a word of truth in it! I appeal to Mrs. Cornett —" exclaimed the discomfited Agnes.

"Mrs. Cornett repeated your remark afterwards to Bertie van Tahn," continued Tobermory, "and said, 'That woman is a regular Hunger Marcher; she'd go anywhere for four square meals a day,' and Bertie van Tahn said —"

At this point the chronicle mercifully ceased. Tobermory had caught a glimpse of the big yellow tom from the rectory working his way through the shrubbery toward the stable wing. In a flash he had vanished through the open French window.

With the disappearance of his too brilliant pupil Cornelius Appin found himself beset by a hurricane of bitter upbraiding, anxious inquiry, and frightened entreaty. The responsibility for the situation lay with him, and he must prevent matters from becoming worse. Could Tober-

mory impart his dangerous gift to other cats? was the first question he had to answer. It was possible, he replied, that he might have initiated his intimate friend the stable puss into his new accomplishment, but it was unlikely that his teaching could have taken a wider range as yet.

"Then," said Mrs. Cornett, "Tobermory may be a valuable cat and a great pet; but I'm sure you'll agree, Adelaide, that both he and the stable cat must be done away with without delay."

"You don't suppose I've enjoyed the last quarter of an hour, do you?" said Lady Blemley bitterly. "My husband and I are very fond of Tobermory — at least, we were before this horrible accomplishment was infused into him; but now, of course, the only thing is to have him destroyed as soon as possible."

"We can put some strychnine in the scraps he always gets at dinnertime," said Sir Wilfrid, "and I will go and drown the stable cat myself. The coachman will be very sore at losing his pet, but I'll say a very catching form of mange has broken out in both cats and we're afraid of spreading it to the kennels."

"But my great discovery!" expostulated Mr. Appin. "After all my years of research and experiment —"

"You can go and experiment on the shorthorns at the farm, who are under proper control," said Mrs. Cornett, "or the elephants at the Zoological Gardens. They're said to be highly intelligent, and they have this recommendation, that they don't come creeping about our bedrooms and under chairs, and so forth."

An archangel ecstatically proclaiming the millennium, and then finding it clashed unpardonably with Henley and would have to be indefinitely postponed, could hardly have felt more crestfallen than Cornelius Appin at the reception of his wonderful achievement. Public opinion, however, was against him; in fact, had the general voice been consulted on the subject it is probable that a strong minority vote would have been in favor of including him in the strychnine diet.

Defective train arrangements and a nervous desire to see matters brought to a finish prevented an immediate dispersal of the party, but dinner that evening was not a social success. Sir Wilfrid had had rather a trying time with the stable cat and subsequently with the coachman. Agnes Resker ostentatiously limited her repast to a morsel of dry toast, which she bit as thought it were a personal enemy; while Mavis Pellington maintained a vindictive silence throughout the meal. Lady Blemley kept up a flow of what she hoped was conversation, but her attention was fixed on the doorway. A plateful of carefully dosed fish scraps was in readiness on the sideboard, but sweets and savory and dessert went their way, and no Tobermory appeared either in the dining room or kitchen.

The sepulchral dinner was cheerful compared with the subsequent vigil in the smoking room. Eating and drinking had at least supplied a distraction and cloak to the prevailing embarrassment. Bridge was out of the question in the general tension of nerves and tempers, and after Odo Finsberry had given a lugubrious rendering of "Melisande in the Wood" to a frigid audience, music was tacitly avoided. At eleven the servants went to bed, announcing that the small window in the pantry had been left open as usual for Tobermory's private use. The guests read steadily through the current batch of magazines, and fell back gradually on the Badminton Library and bound volumes of *Punch*. Lady Blemley made periodic visits to the pantry, returning each time with an expression of listless depression which forestalled questioning.

At two o'clock Clovis broke the dominating silence.

"He won't turn up tonight. He's probably in the local newspaper office at the present moment, dictating the first installment of reminiscences. Lady What's-her-name's book won't be in it. It will be the event of the day."

Having made this contribution to the general cheerfulness, Clovis went to bed. At long intervals the various members of the house party followed his example.

The servants taking round the early tea made a uniform announcement in reply to a

uniform question. Tobermory had not returned.

Breakfast was, if anything, a more unpleasant function than dinner had been, but before its conclusion the situation was relieved. Tobermory's corpse was brought in from the shrubbery, where a gardener had just discovered it. From the bites on his throat and the yellow fur which coated his claws it was evident that he had fallen in unequal combat with the big tom from the rectory.

By midday most of the guests had quitted the Towers, and after lunch Lady Blemley had sufficiently recovered her spirits to write an extremely nasty letter to the rectory about the loss of her valuable pet.

Tobermory had been Appin's one successful pupil, and he was destined to have no successor. A few weeks later an elephant in the Dresden Zoological Garden, which had shown no previous signs of irritability, broke loose and killed an Englishman who had apparently been teasing it. The victim's name was variously reported in the papers as Oppin and Eppelin, but his front name was faithfully rendered Cornelius.

"If he was trying German irregular verbs on the poor beast," said Clovis, "he deserved all he got."

LITTLE WHITE KING

Spring vanished with the blossom, and summer loitered imperceptibly into autumn. The sycamores clung to their leaves, then, in two or three sudden gusts, let them down on the lawns. He found a new delight: that of following the gardener as he swung the arc of the broom across and across the grass. Sometimes he became a white windmill, a catherine-wheel of silver, cutting indescribable capers among the dry brown flakes that broke into confetti on his back, his flanks and the banner of his tail. Always addicted to the mower, he helped to give the lawns their last cut of the year.

All who had known him from his infancy remarked upon the burgeoning of his beauty, during those autumnal weeks. 'In standing water' between kitten and cat, his adolescence, like that of the human animal, had a poignancy of its own, which one knew

STEEN

69

must vanish when his transformation was complete. He had grown enormously; from the tip of his nose to the base of his tail he was already longer than the Black One, although not quite so tall. The tail had lost the very last of its pale golden trace, and was broader than the broadest ostrich plume. His feet no longer seemed too big for his body, and had garnished themselves with a set of powerful nails, more like jade than ivory, which he still employed too often on upholstery, but never on those who played with him. If, by misfortune, they missed their mark — the piece of ribbon or paper or string we were trailing for him — and registered on human flesh, it was never his intention; the torn hand, offered in place of the toy, was patted with a pad of velvet.

He was very imperious; very definite and autocratic in his requirements. He really needed a vassal, dedicated to his service alone: to shut and open doors, give him a drop of milk, dry his paws when he had been out in the rain, find the ping-pong balls he always batted into the most inaccessible places, or carry him on a shoulder. Although it was easy to say he was 'always eating' (a couple of mouthfuls at a time), no thickness developed in the soft, elastic body, no hardness in the tender bones. To lift him was still like lifting a muff. I wondered how long the sweet sensation would last. He must harden, grow sinewy, develop the rangy stride of the male and the predatory head of the hunter. Of one thing I was glad: the loss of his sex had not affected his vocal cords; his cry, his purr still had the richness of the entire.

One thing in particular endeared him to me: his almost benign attitude towards birds. Full of interest and curiosity, he stalked them, but never — at least in my sight — attempted to kill them. He followed the foolish feathered things through grass or border, flattening himself, watching with sparkling eyes, but never, apparently, with lethal intent. He appeared to extend to them the innocent attention he gave to all small moving objects — leaves, butterflies or shadows. He leapt, he struck. If the blow had ever landed, one can hardly doubt that primitive instinct would have asserted itself; but somehow, for all his agility, he always missed, and, missing, lost interest in the game.

The same with field mice. Never having had to hunt for his food, he was content to give them a pat or two, and could seldom be troubled to follow them when they escaped into the long grass. I must confess to feeling rather badly about this: something like a mother whose small boy fails to distinguish himself in the field of sport; but consoled myself by reflecting on his many gifts and graces, which more sportsmanlike cats could not rival. I remembered one of my little North Country queens, a loving little party, who almost every morning brought me in a cold, dead mouse, which she laid on my pillow and nozzled affectionately up against my ear, in case I should overlook it; it was a compliment with which one could dispense — and one which might well have occurred to le Petit Roi if he had been a mouser. I had been spared something — if only the sight of mutilated little bodies, which, vermin though they be, give me a horrid pang.

When winter declared itself, with fogs and frosts and raw, cheerless mornings, he spent more time indoors, making still closer acquaintance of the human beings who guarded his simple life.

He had no specially favored spot for his repose; sometimes it was at the head of the stairs, close to a radiator. Sometimes it was on the dining-room hearthrug, in front of the Pither stove, or on one of the Napoleon chairs in the corners of the fireside. On sunny mornings it was in the deep alcove of a little window, between a Frank Dobson model of a child's head and the sun-warmed glass. Sometimes it was the dressing stool in front of my looking-glass, with the electric stove behind him. At night, when we gathered in the parlor, it was the back of a couch, or under the flounce of a chair. Unlike the Black One, he did not care for cushions, or any too-yielding surface; I had learned, when he came on my bed, to push back the eiderdown and make a little flat space for him on the mattress, where, after conducting his toilet, he settled to sleep.

One thing he had in common with the Black One: a mania for the social life. Christmas, with an influx of guests, was bliss — from the dinner party on Christmas Eve to the Twelfth

Night cocktail. It was not only a wild and whirling time of tinsel and cellophane, sparkles and ribbons, things that went bang and flashed (his first experience of drawing-room fireworks brought him near swooning point with ecstasy); but he was the center of attention — the Snow King, the Winter King, *le petit roi Noel!*

He received tributes with dignified reserve, resisted some foolish attempts to interest him in his Christmas cards and, sated at last with pleasure, folded his paws under his chest, to watch the goings-ons. His best Christmas present, a mechanical mouse, he played with on Christmas Eve, showing, I fear, more politeness than enthusiasm, and thereafter abandoned. Human beings, with their strange and unpredictable antics, were more fun than a clockwork mouse. His aloofness made the Black One's eager friendliness and her readiness to show off her self-taught tricks appear — alas — almost fulsome.

He and the Black One had arrived, by then, at 'an understanding.' It was his doing, not hers. But she, with all her elderly ways, her natural anxiety to retain the first place in my affection, was not proof against a little pink muzzle that lifted itself to hers, the soft persistence of his approach, the warmth and comfort of that silver fleece on a winter night. They had begun occasionally to share an armchair: the Black One reluctant, taut, drawn into herself and stiff with resistance, he folded calmly, seemingly immovable, but encroaching little by little on her space, on the woolen scarf that belonged to her, until their limbs were touching. The Black One flung agonized glances at me: 'Must I bear this?' I nodded. The Black One sighed and accepted the all but imperceptible contact. She drew the line, however, on the one occasion he attempted to wash her. What? — a miniature poodle with four champions in her pedigree — submit to being washed by a cat? She bit him, for once, in earnest — and justifiably; and the lesson did him no harm. He sat, blinking offendedly; but, in that respect, he sinned no more. Even when he chewed the tassels on her ears, he showed, thereafter, a certain awareness of the 'thus far and no farther' — which he was keen enough on claiming for himself.

As the days darkened, and there was little to tempt him out of doors, he developed a regime

73

of his own. In the mornings he shadowed Alice about her household duties. Sometimes on her shoulder, sometimes under her arm, he helped her to dust, to sweep and polish — pouncing with delight on the duster, taking flying leaps on to the tops of cupboards or dressers; finally settling on plate-chest or sideboard, his tail curled round his toes, admiring his own reflection in the shining surface. When he endangered something fragile or precious with his antics, Alice's reproachful 'Bert!' was an endearment. When I picked him up in my arms, and, instead of giving him the spanking he had earned, called him 'My white tom kitten!' his struggles and flounces to escape were tolerated for the sake of his perfect beauty.

One of the things most beguiling, to cat-lovers, is the intractability of a cat, its blank refusal of coercion, its refusal to surrender the least part of its spiritual independence even to those for whom it has learned to care. No one who does not understand and accept this is fit to have the guardianship of a cat. Only one cat of my acquaintance, a Mrs. Bertha Mocatta, was amenable to physical punishment; but Mrs. B. was a gorgeous old tavern harridan who took from her owner the cosh she constantly earned as merely one of the courtesies of everyday existence, and was capable to her last sinful breath of fighting back. Idolizing the hand that obliged her to behave herself, Mrs. B. was one of the immortals; for some time after her demise, her presence was (literally) felt in the studio over which she ruled after her previous owners gave up the local in which she was raised. Her ghost would still be around, I think, but for the establishment of her successor, the gentle Mrs. Laura Chevely, against whom ghostly teeth and ghostly talons cannot prevail.

It may have been noticed that I use the word 'guardianship' in preference to 'ownership,' of a cat. 'Ownership' implies authority over body and soul. A dog, in its devotion, will of its own free will, accept this authority; a cat, never. This independence is offensive to people who do not care for cats: I have never been able to understand why. I can no more see why one should assume possession over an animal than over a human being.

Now that winter had come, le Petit Roi's afternoons were passed in sleep, unless a brief

74

gleam of sun enticed him out of doors, or the northerly gale, fluttering the dead leaves, tempted him to fling himself about the lawns. He would visit our neighbors, trotting across their grass, lifting his little head, uttering his beguiling Prr-rr-oo, and wave his tail in acknowledgment of a caress, before leaping up their pergola, or on the garage roof, or into the pear tree, where he stood out on a branch, noble as a ship's figurehead, breasting the gale; or, up on the ridge tiles, allowed himself to be blown into a white chrysanthemum by the wind.

His communications with those who shared the house with him now notably increased their range. When he looked up and observed 'Pr-rr-oo,' he was not asking for food, or to go out, or to be played with. It was 'I am here' or 'Where have you been?' or simply 'Take notice of me.' Often he came and sat beside me, on the arm of chair or sofa, purring so loudly that the Black One would rouse and lift her head in astonishment.

He discovered the miracle of the fires; tempting as they were, he was very sensible about them. For all the comfort they gave him, he was careful not to singe his coat or the restless plume of his tail. And, cozy as he found them, he would withdraw himself — though with an air of protest — if the person he wished to be with was not sitting near the fire.

In one manner he was implacable, and, as the evening wore on, impatient. He must have his games. Useless to offer him his ping-pong balls, his string with the rabbit's tail on the end of it, his crumpled bits of silver paper or the bells that swung on the Black One's collar and lead. He flatly refused to play by himself. He sulked, set up a protestant yowl; leapt on the card table, to scatter aces and kings and queens, and to pat the pencil of the score card on to the floor. Dismissed as a nuisance, he set out on a gloomy progress over chairs, tables and sofas; he deliberately attacked the screen of cordobes leather, or the newly covered couch — anything that was precious and would bring some one leaping to check his ill behavior.

There was nothing for it but to play with him; to rush up and down stairs, trailing a scarf, or the Black One's lead. The game hurtled from room to room; he crouched under beds, to leap out with a wild pat at our ankles; he flung himself prone in affected exhaustion belied by the wild, dark brightness of his eyes. Sometimes the exhaustion was real, and he submitted to being thrown over one's shoulder like a white tippet, and rocked backwards and forwards, purring quietly — until, at the moment one fondly believed he was falling asleep, he would take a bound like a flying squirrel, and the game was on again.

One day shortly after Christmas he had a shock.

At twilight, I opened the back door to let him out, and as he took a cautious step on to the porch, the air around him filled itself with white feathers. The whirling whiteness took him by surprise; he drew back, then, losing his head completely, turned round and flew straight up into my arms. I laughed and held him, and walked out with him on to the path. The snow fell on him and me, and because I was holding him he recovered his confidence, and presently leapt lightly down and went to his accustomed place on the border. But for once he did not linger. It was too cold. He flashed past me, rushed to the dining-room fire, and began hurriedly to lick the cold wetness that had settled on his coat.

Next morning, sitting on the bench at my bedroom window, he looked out on a strange world: a scene of whiteness, glittering with sun. He was fascinated. Presently he called to be let out, and slid on to the back porch, which had been swept clear, and was already warmed by the eastern sun. He sat there, taking in the altered aspect of his familiar surroundings. After watching le Petit Roi gazing at the greenness which overnight had been translated into whiteness, I have no doubt that cats know about color. He was baffled and impressed.

The flagged path that leads down under the archway and out into the lane had also been swept, and, at his own leisure, he trotted down it, for another view of this strange, white scene.

Meanwhile, the Black One had gone for her morning walk. She had known many snows and, on the whole, enjoyed them. Her minute feet, hardly bigger than bird's claws, sank into the cold softness, she rubbed her muzzle in the snow and came up with white moustaches and fringes of white on her ears. As le Petit Roi sat there, under the archway, she returned up the lane.

He rose on his toes; he blew himself out into a white balloon; he spat — for the first time in his life. He swayed back into a defensive arc, as IT came by: a black and yellow IT, familiar, yet horribly strange. The Black One, in her daffodil-yellow sweater which he had never seen before, horrified him. He slapped out a paw. The Black One stood still and stared. He hunched himself, let out a slow, protracted growl, and spat again. The Black One, impressed, walked up for a closer view of this strange conduct on the part of one who, so far, had never been anything but amiable.

His eyes blackened and enlarged themselves, his pink mouth, wide open, dragged back at the corners, held in his breath. Then, with a gasp, he recognized the Black One, and shot like an arrow for the kitchen door. Shaking the snow from her fringes, the Black One galloped after him. They hunched at each other in front of the dining-room stove, then spent ten minutes smelling each other all over from head to tail, as though meeting for the first time.

That was the week he discovered the possibilities of the Knole couch. The last, most lovely picture of the Little King is of a long white arm, reaching between the back and the slung end of the couch; of a snow-white head, mad with gaiety, and a pair of ruby-red eyes blazing from shadow at the evening paper, rolled up and poked into the space between cushions and wall for him to snatch at.

It was round about that time that I wrote in my diary:

'Of all the cats that have owned me, there has never been one like my white tom kitten, for sweetness, intelligence and affection. Hearing is very unimportant after all.'

DICK BAKER'S CAT

One of my comrades there — another of those victims of eighteen years of unrequited toil and blighted hopes — was one of the gentlest spirits that ever bore its patient cross in a weary exile; grave and simple Dick Baker, pocket miner of Dead-Horse Gulch. He was forty-six, gray as a rat, earnest, thoughtful, slenderly educated, slouchily dressed, and clay-soiled, but his heart was finer metal than any gold his shovel ever brought to light — than any, indeed, that ever was mined or minted.

Whenever he was out of luck and a little downhearted, he would fall to mourning over the loss of a wonderful cat he used to own (for where women and children are not, men of kindly impulses take up with pets, for they must love something). And he always spoke of the strange sagacity of that cat with the air of a man who believed in his secret heart that there

TWAIN

TWAIN

was something human about it — maybe even supernatural.

I heard him talking about this animal once. He said: "Gentlemen, I used to have a cat here, by the name of Tom Quartz, which you'd 'a' took an interest in, I reckon — most anybody would. I had him here eight year — and he was the remarkablest cat *I* ever see. He was a large gray one of the Tom specie, an' he had more hard, natchral sense than any man in this camp — 'n' a *power* of dignity — he wouldn't let the Gov'ner of Californy be familiar with him. He never ketched a rat in his life — 'peared to be above it. He never cared for nothing but mining. He knowed more about mining, that cat did, than any man *I* ever, ever see. You couldn't tell *him* noth'n' 'bout placer-diggin's — 'n' as for pocket mining, why he was just born for it. He would dig out after me an' Jim when we went over the hills prospect'n', and he would trot along behind us for as much as five mile, if we went so fur. An' he had the best judgment about mining ground — why, you never see anything like it. When we went to work, he'd scatter a glance round, 'n' if he didn' think much of the indications, he would give a look as much as to say, 'Well, I'll have to get you to excuse *me*' — 'n' without another word he'd hyste his nose in the air 'n' shove for home. But if the ground suited him, he would lay low 'n' keep dark till the first pan was washed, 'n' then he would sidle up 'n' take a look, an' if there was about six or seven grains of gold *he* was satisfied — he didn't want no better prospect 'n' that — 'n' then he would lay down on our coats and snore like a steamboat till we'd struck the pocket, an' then get up 'n' superintend. He was nearly lightnin' on superintending.

"Well, by an' by, up comes this yer quartz excitement. Everybody was into it — everybody was pick'n' 'n' blast'n' instead of shovelin' dirt on the hillside — everybody was putt'n' down a shaft instead of scrapin' the surface. Noth'n' would do Jim, but *we* must tackle the ledges, too, 'n' so we did. We commenced putt'n' down a shaft, 'n' Tom Quartz he begin to wonder what in the dickens it was all about. *He* hadn't ever seen any mining like that before, 'n' he was all upset, as you may say — he couldn't come to a right understanding of it no way — it was too many for *him*. He was down on it too, you bet you — he was down on it pow-

80

erful — 'n' always appeared to consider it the cussedest foolishness out. But that cat, you know, was *always* agin' newfangled arrangements — somehow he never could abide 'em. *You* know how it is with old habits. But by and by Tom Quartz begin to git sort of reconciled a little though he never *could* altogether understand that eternal sinkin' of a shaft an' never pannin' out anything. At last he got to comin' down in the shaft, hisself, to try to cipher it out. An' when he'd git the blues, 'n' feel kind o' scruffy, 'n' aggravated 'n' disgusted — knowin' as he did, that the bills was runnin' up all the time an' we warn't makin' a cent — he would curl up on a gunnysack in the corner an' go to sleep. Well, one day when the shaft was down about eight foot, the rock got so hard that we had to put in a blast — the first blast'n' we'd ever done since Tom Quartz was born. An' then we lit the fuse 'n' clumb out 'n' got off 'bout fifty yards — 'n' forgot 'n' left Tom Quartz sound asleep on the gunnysack. In 'bout a minute we seen a puff of smoke bust up out of the hole, 'n' then everything let go with an awful crash, 'n about four million ton of rocks 'n' dirt 'n' smoke 'n' splinters shot up 'bout a mile an' a half into the air, an' by George, right in the dead center of it was old Tom Quartz a-goin' end over end, an' a-snortin' an' a-sneezin', an' a-clawin' an' a-reach'n' for things like all possessed. But it warn't no use, you know, it warn't no use. An' that was the last we see of *him* for about two minutes 'n' a half, an' then all of a sudden it begin to rain rocks and rubbage an' directly he come down ker-whoop about ten foot off f'm where we stood. Well, I reckon he was p'r'aps the orneriest-lookin' beast you ever see. One ear was sot back on his neck, 'n' his tail was stove up, 'n' his eye-winkers was singed off, 'n' he was all blacked up with powder an' smoke, an' all sloppy with mud 'n' slush f'm one end to the other. Well, sir, it warn't no use to try to apologize — we couldn't say a word. He took a sort of disgusted look at himself, 'n' then he looked at us — an' it was just exactly the same as if he had said — 'Gents, maybe *you* think it's smart to take advantage of a cat that ain't had no experience of quartz minin', but *I* think different' — an' then he turned on his heel 'n' marched off home without ever saying another word.

"That was jest his style. An' maybe you won't believe it, but after that you never see a cat

so prejudiced agin' quartz mining as what he was. An' by an' by when he *did* get to goin' down in the shaft agin', you'd 'a' been astonished at his sagacity. The minute we'd tetch off a blast 'n' the fuse'd begin to sizzle, he'd give a look as much as to say, 'Well, I'll have to git you to excuse *me*,' an' it was surpris'n' the way he'd shin out of that hole 'n' go f'r a tree. Sagacity? It ain't no name for it. 'Twas inspiration!"

I said, "Well, Mr. Baker, his prejudice against quartz mining *was* remarkable, considering how he came by it. Couldn't you ever cure him of it?"

"*Cure him*! No! When Tom Quartz was sot once, he was *always* sot — and you might 'a' blowed him up as much as three million times 'n' you'd never 'a' broken him of his cussed prejudice agin' quartz mining."

THE PARADISE OF CATS

An aunt bequeathed me an Angora cat, which is certainly the most stupid animal I know of. This is what my cat related to me, one winter night, before the warm embers.

I

I was then two years old, and I was certainly the fattest and most simple cat anyone could have seen. Even at that tender age I displayed all the presumption of an animal that scorns the attractions of the fireside. And yet what gratitude I owed to Providence for having placed me with your aunt! The worthy woman idolized me. I had a regular bedroom at the bottom of a cupboard, with a feather pillow and a triple-folded rug. The food was as good as the bed; no bread or soup, nothing but meat, good underdone meat.

Well! amidst all these comforts, I had but one wish, but one dream, to slip out by the half-open window, and run away on to the tiles. Caresses appeared to me insipid, the softness of my bed disgusted me, I was so fat that I felt sick, and from morn till eve I experienced the weariness of being happy.

I must tell you that by straining my neck I had perceived the opposite roof from the window. That day four cats were fighting there. With bristling coats and tails in the air, they were rolling on the blue slates, in the full sun, amidst oaths of joy. I had never witnessed such an extraordinary sight. From that moment my convictions were settled. Real happiness was upon that roof, in front of that window which the people of the house so carefully closed. I found the proof of this in the way in which they shut the doors of the cupboards where the meat was hidden.

I made up my mind to fly. I felt sure there were other things in life than underdone meat. There was the unknown, the ideal. One day they forgot to close the kitchen window. I sprang on to a small roof beneath it.

II

How beautiful the roofs were! They were bordered by broad gutters exhaling delicious odors. I followed those gutters in raptures of delight, my feet sinking into fine mud, which was deliciously warm and soft. I fancied I was walking on velvet. And the generous heat of the sun melted my fat.

I will not conceal from you the fact that I was trembling in every limb. My delight was mingled with terror. I remember, particularly, experiencing a terrible shock that almost made me tumble down into the street. Three cats came rolling over from the top of a house towards me, mewing most frightfully, and as I was on the point of fainting away, they called me a silly thing, and said they were mewing for fun. I began mewing with them. It was charming. The jolly fellows had none of my stupid fat. When I slipped on the sheets of zinc heated by the burning sun, they laughed at me. An old tom, who was one of the band, showed me par-

ticular friendship. He offered to teach me a thing or two, and I gratefully accepted. Ah! your aunt's cat's meat was far from my thoughts! I drank in the gutters, and never had sugared milk seemed so sweet to me. Everything appeared nice and beautiful. A she-cat passed by, a charming she-cat, the sight of her gave me a feeling I had never experienced before. Hitherto, I had only seen these exquisite creatures, with such delightfully supple backbones, in my dreams. I and my three companions rushed forward to meet the newcomer. I was in front of the others, and was about to pay my respects to the bewitching thing, when one of my comrades cruelly bit my neck. I cried out with pain.

"Bah!" said the old tom, leading me away; "you will meet with stranger adventures than that."

III

After an hour's walk I felt as hungry as a wolf.

"What do you eat on the roofs?" I inquired of my friend the tom.

"What you can find," he answered shrewdly.

This reply caused me some embarrassment, for though I carefully searched I found nothing. At last I perceived a young work-girl in a garret preparing her lunch. A beautiful chop of a tasty red color was lying on a table under the window.

"There's the very thing I want," I thought, in all simplicity.

And I sprang on to the table and took the chop. But the work girl, having seen me, struck me a fearful blow with a broom on the spine, and I fled, uttering a dreadful oath.

"You are fresh from your village then?" said the tom. "Meat that is on tables is there for the purpose of being longed for at a distance. You must search in the gutters."

I could never understand that kitchen meat did not belong to cats. My stomach was beginning to get seriously angry. The tom put me completely to despair by telling me it would be necessary to wait until night. Then we would go down into the street and turn over the heaps of muck. Wait until night! He said it quietly, like a hardened philosopher. I felt myself fainting at the mere thought of this prolonged fast.

IV

Night came slowly, a foggy night that chilled me to the bones. It soon began to rain, a fine, penetrating rain, driven by sudden gusts of wind. We went down along the glazed roof of a staircase. How ugly the street appeared to me! It was no longer that nice heat, that beautiful sun, those roofs white with light where one rolled about so deliciously. My paws slipped on the greasy stones. I sorrowfully recalled to memory my triple blanket and feather pillow.

We were hardly in the street when my friend the tom began to tremble. He made himself small, very small, and ran stealthily along beside the houses, telling me to follow as rapidly as possible. He rushed in at the first street door he came to, and purred with satisfaction as he sought refuge there. When I questioned him as to the motive of his flight, he answered:

"Did you see that man with a basket on his back and a stick with an iron hook at the end?"

"Yes."

"Well! if he had seen us he would have knocked us on the heads and roasted us!"

"Roasted us!" I exclaimed. "Then the street is not ours? One can't eat, but one's eaten!"

V

However, the boxes of kitchen refuse had been emptied before the street doors. I rummaged in the heaps in despair. I came across two or three bare bones that had been lying among the cinders, and I then understood what a succulent dish fresh cat's meat made. My friend the tom scratched artistically among the muck. He made me run about until morning, inspecting each heap, and without showing the least hurry. I was out in the rain for more than ten hours, shivering in every limb. Cursed street, cursed liberty, and how I regretted my prison!

At dawn the tom, seeing I was staggering said to me with a strange air:

"Have you had enough of it?"

"Oh yes," I answered.

"Do you want to go home?"

"I do, indeed; but how shall I find the house?"

"Come along. This morning, when I saw you come out, I understood that a fat cat like you was not made for the lively delights of liberty. I know your place of abode and will take you to the door."

The worthy tom said this very quietly. When we had arrived, he bid me "Good-bye," without betraying the least emotion.

"No," I exclaimed, "we will not leave each other so. You must accompany me. We will share the same bed and the same food. My mistress is a good woman — "

He would not allow me to finish my sentence.

"Hold your tongue," he said sharply, "you are a simpleton. Your effeminate existence would kill me. Your life of plenty is good for bastard cats. Free cats would never purchase your cat's meat and feather pillow at the price of a prison. Good-bye."

And he returned up on to the roofs, where I saw his long outline quiver with joy in the rays of the rising sun.

When I got in, your aunt took the whip and gave me a thrashing which I received with profound delight. I tasted in full measure the pleasure of being beaten and being warm. Whilst she was striking me, I thought with rapture of the meat she would give me afterwards.

* * *

You see — concluded my cat, stretching itself out in front of the embers — real happiness, paradise, my dear master, consists in being shut up and beaten in a room where there is meat.

I am speaking from the point of view of cats.